The Tribe That Discovered Trust
How trust is created lost and regained in commercial interactions

David Amerland

NewLine Publishing

The Tribe That Discovered Trust

Printed in the United States of America.

First Printing, 2015

ISBN 13: 978-1-84481-976-8

ISBN 10: 1-84481-976-0

Published by: New Line Publishing

Interior Design by: NuType of Boulder, Colorado

Cover Design by: NR Graphics

Editing by: Samantha Wales

Warning and Disclaimer

Content at a Glance

Contents

"Trust Agents are digital natives using the web to be genuine and to humanize their business. they are interested in people (prospective customers, employees, colleagues, and more) and they have realized that these tools that enable more unique, robust communication also allow more business opportunities for everyone".
- Trust Agents

About the Author

David Amerland is the author of nine best-selling books on search, social media and marketing, including *Google Semantic Search*, *SEO Help* and *The Social Media Mind*.

His involvement with the Web goes back to the days when the number of websites in existence could fit in a printed 80-page directory and SEO consisted of keyword stuffing and pixel-wide hidden text.

Since those less enlightened days he has worked with blue-chip multinationals and individual entrepreneurs alike helping them craft SEO and social media marketing strategies that work with their internal cultures and deliver value to their target audience.

He writes for Forbes, HP UK, Social Media Today, and blogs on his own website, davidamerland.com. When he is not writing or surfing the Web he spends time giving speeches on how social media is changing everything.

Dedication

Every person needs an anchor. I am no different. There are two Ns in my life and in their own way each helps keep me sane and grounded, at least while they are looking. To them both I am beholden.

Acknowledgments

Every book I write makes me conscious of just how many people exactly it takes to help me do something only I can do. The list is long for this one too. Heidi Bouman has to be first not just because without her keeping order in the Cloudwars community I would not have been able to concentrate but because she also managed to keep track of every single Unicorn! Full kudos to John Kellden whose sensemaking has always made sense and who has been instrumental in unleashing more thoughts than most people I know. Iblis Bane needs a mention, not least because he made me realize that trust has nothing to do with a name and a picture. A special thanks to Bruce Marko, who gets what trust is about and Ron Serina, whose conversations are always enjoyable. In putting this book together I drew from my own well of ideas but I could not have plumbed those depths so well had I not known Vincent Messina who really needs to be experienced over time to be appreciated. I am more grateful than I could ever let you know to all those I cannot mention in the companies I work with. Your generous sharing of data, ideas and stories of success and failure helped me shape a book that's relevant to what we are trying to achieve in the 21st century. A special mention must be made to Jared Hamilton, CEO at DrivingSales for generously sharing original research in the automobile industry, there are few organizations that get just how important trust is in closing the gap between a brand and its customers and these guys really get it. The illustration included in the first chapter of the third section of this book is directly from their research. There are two more people I am going to single out this time. One is Oleg Moskalensky whose conversation, ideas and above all friendship always make me feel more worthy than I have a right to be. The other one is Farinaz Parsay whose candor is always captivating. This list is not exhaustive by any means and there are many more I have not singled out. You're on G+ and we talk often. To you all I am particularly grateful and you know who you are. Finally thanks to Samantha Wales for putting up with my last minute changes and my tardiness in returning the edits. As always, many more eyes than just mine have looked at this manuscript and suggested changes and corrections. The mistakes that might persist, are down to yours truly.

Introduction

The world has changed. Technology is driving a large part of that change but it is not the reason for the change itself. Technology, of itself, continues to do what it has always done: in the first instance it provides an amplification of our physical capabilities that changes the physical restrictions the world imposes upon us. Then, as it matures, it picks up and amplifies the invisible things inside our heads, the space where our thoughts, desires and hopes swirl. In doing so it begins to merge the impact of both function and form. It breaches the traditional barriers that contain us and brings what's inside our heads outside and vice versa.

That's when it really challenges us because it forces us to try and understand the things we have never really thought about. The things we tend to take for granted: Trust and trustworthiness, truth and truthfulness, honesty and reputation. Being good as opposed to being bad. As it becomes embedded into our lives technology becomes invisible, but its effects are still felt.

The world, we say, has become more transparent. It's technology that has made it so. Social media platforms have changed the way we communicate with one another and they've changed the way we receive information from those who traditionally have been the gatekeepers of power in our world. They have changed the way we find romantic partners, jobs and friends. They've changed the way we form communities and create modern tribes.

The devices in our pockets have become so powerful and capable that we barely think about what they do. We just know that they are there. Capable of bringing people together, across countries, ethnicities, timezones and language barriers.

That's the paradox about technology. In the early days when you're struggling to get it to do what you want it to do, it's all about the technology. When that is taken care of however. When devices just work. When data flows everywhere, unbidden, unstoppable, with the barest of friction. When information conforms to the vision famously formalized by Stewart Brand and actually is free because the cost of sharing it is so low as to be virtually zero. Then technology disappears entirely. What is important when this happens is what has always been important: Human relationships.

That's when we begin to realize that while things are still the same some things have changed. We form relationships when we have no choice because we physically have to exist. We have to have a shape and a form and it needs a place to live in and another place to work and both of these places are surrounded by other shapes and forms, similar to ours with which we need to find ways to get along.

In the digital domain however we always have a choice. We choose to be online and we choose to do specific things when there. We choose the people we talk to and decide just how we want to be known and what we really want to be.

While all this may sound as artifice, it's anything but. We cannot start to create anything we are unfamiliar with. Most of us find it hard to impersonate a member of the opposite sex and we are far more familiar with them than we are with any other concept.

What we are and what we become in a world where we send the digital equivalent of an astral projection of ourselves is directly rooted in who we are and what we believe in, it stems from the bricks and mortar world that first gave us birth and taught us about the principles we find important.

That's how we begin to gradually think more analytically about how we go about constructing a more faithful 'us' – a better digital avatar than even our flesh and blood selves. All too often, in the 'real world' where mental bandwidth is restricted by biology and things happen in a more localized, immediate way, we give in to the hormonal tides that wash our biological systems. Emotions such as anger, fear and disgust take over faster than we can control our actions and we frequently react in ways that lock us into stereotypical ways of engagement and interaction.

In the digital domain however we are a little bit different. More augmented. More connected. Our emotions are tempered by distance and time. Our knowledge is enhanced by the people we know and the things they do. Some of our interactions happen asynchronously. Much of our engagement happens publicly. And we are always amplified in our capacity by the power of search whose learned retrieval of information makes our arguments deeper and our responses more balanced.

In the digital domain everything is a multi-layered construct, built carefully and painstakingly. Invested in heavily and usually after some thought. Because the technology that connects us is invisible and ubiquitous we learn to analyze the connections we make and understand the value of engagement and interaction.

We learn how reputations are built and authority is created. We see how trust is born, shared, propagated, lost and regained. Rather than stripping us of our humanity our digital selves strip our humanity from its unthinking, instinctive reactions and force us to become more thoughtful in our actions. More considerate in our choices. More reaching in our ambitions and further seeing in our planning.

Many of us, by degrees, become a little better in the flesh and blood, bricks and mortar world, because we have been exposed to kindness and intelligence as well as pain and stupidity in our online existence.

Our digital selves, in return, constantly evolve. Our understanding of the dynamics of networks and the digital realm is increasing all the time. Our stores of data get richer and our reams of analysis get deeper and we learn more and more what works and what doesn't, and why.

In writing a book on Trust, how it's born, how it's propagated and why, I faced a dilemma: how to show the human element in a book that's devoted to looking at a very human, very fundamental quality in a very cold, analytical and data-driven way.

More than that, I wanted to show how by understanding how trust works, what it is and how to gain it we can actually become more honest instead of less so. Of course, as with every other human activity it is true that knowing how something works we can try to emulate it, taking on its characteristics, applying its components even when we neither feel nor deserve what it depicts.

If it was that easy to fake trust we'd be doing it already. It's true that in any short-term, isolated moment trustworthiness can be faked quite successfully. The real world has a much higher level of data density than the digital one. Just meeting someone at a party, for example, allows us to gauge the way they dress, listen to the way they speak, determine their level of education and social status, assess their importance – and decide whether we like them or not, without even exchanging a single word with them.

In the real world we can be tricked by conmen and fooled by people whose intent is to fool us. But not for long. Not all the time. And not all of us. The online world is more porous, transparent and connected than the offline one. Pretending to be something there when you're not becomes even harder.

Stripped of many of the things that are part of who you are in the offline world, online everything you do is informed even more of who you are and what you want to achieve than in the offline one. There are always more eyes on us than we think. If there is no alignment of our core values and our online persona then our online responses will be inconsistent, our online presence will raise red flags and we will soon find ourselves isolated, cut-off, struggling with a reputation that is the antithesis of what we were trying to build.

Does the online world make us automatically more honest? No, but as it is shaping up, its increased level of interconnectivity, transparency and relational analysis, is making it harder for us to be dishonest.

Much of what we experience as 'bad' behavior is the result of human economic behavioral tendencies, our hardwired impulse to look for shortcuts in everything. By definition a shortcut is a path that gives us the same outcome as a much longer one thereby saving us a lot of energy and effort.

We live in the age of the semantic web. Semantic search is constantly mining relationships and ascribing interaction values to people, organizations and things. Semantic technologies are constantly surfacing information looking for trustworthy sources to use as a benchmark.

In the connected age we live in it is important to understand that in order to get anywhere a fictitious entity needs to go into as much trouble and spend as much time and effort as a real one. There is no shortcut. So you may as well do the right thing from the beginning.

Trying to solve my dilemma on humanity I came upon the idea of a tale. We have used narratives, always, to teach ourselves the things we mustn't forget. The things that are important to us. My idea of a tribe came from many conversations with friends and colleagues. With my fictional creation I was able to hide in their belief system, their interactions and engagement with a potential enemy all the human foibles that mark the relationships we form.

The story of trust is one of technology – that much is made abundantly clear in the second section of this book. But it is a quintessentially human story too. The first part is what makes this evident. And it is most probably from that part that some of the most important lessons will come.

Good luck.

David,
Athens

The Tribe

Once upon a time there was a tribe living at the edge of the world. It was not a very big tribe but the world was not very big and in it, this tribe was a very successful one. Because the tribe lived in a very tough territory it had very little competition. Over the years, it managed to build a reputation for producing tough fighting men, always ready for a scrap and that meant that other tribes left it alone.

If things had remained as they were the tribe could have gone on for a very long time, living off the land and hunting and foraging, maintaining its reputation by turning up now and then at solstice festivals when all the tribes would gather for the young warriors to measure themselves up against each other and the young girls to find husbands. But things very rarely remain the same.

The world changes fast. Word was that tribes in other parts were banding together. Growing larger. Because they no longer had to wait for the solstice festivals each year for the girls to find husbands they grew faster still. The young warriors in their midst no longer had to fight to prove themselves worthy. With a steady supply of women the warriors in other tribes looked for other skills that would help them prove themselves. Besides, once married being a warrior was not sufficient to keep a young wife happy. You needed to have a real job, a career of sorts even.

So, some of the former warriors became farmers and produced more and more food, enough not just to feed their own large and growing tribes but also a surplus which they could now trade with other tribes. Trade brought them the need for ledgers to record everything in, and ledgers brought them the need for learning and learning started languages as they realized the value of the knowledge hidden inside the heads of people in other tribes.

Languages brought diplomacy and diplomacy brought fresh contact and more trade and more marriages and more people and fewer warrior and more farmers. Farming however is a slow, steady business. You just don't go from producing no food to producing a surplus in a day, or even a year.

The needs that arose from the strain on resources as the size of these tribes grew also gave rise to ingenuity and innovation. New ways of doing old things were found and this provided farmers and their tribes with fresh ways to use resources and they grew and grew and grew in size until the old ways of the past where tribes would meet and ritually fight so their young warriors could gain experience in fighting and gain reputation and find women and have families so the tribe could prosper, appeared useless, inefficient and strangely barbaric and were eventually abandoned. Trade now ruled supreme.

That was how things were in the middle of the world.

At the edge of the world however, news traveled slowly. A hunter would meet an old friend from another tribe out hunting, and they would exchange news. There would be a trader who would make the arduous journey to the edge and bring with him examples of wonderful inventions the tribe had never heard of.

The rumors of what was happening did not seem to affect them. The words of the traders who occasionally found them appeared insubstantial, forgotten the moment the trader was out of sight.

Life at the edge of the world, it was felt, could go on forever.

Chapter 1

Contact

Pugna was the leader. As a leader he was strong and brave and he always led from the front. Obeo and Hiemo were in line behind him. Fugae brought up the rear. The tribe had a troupe of four because this was the optimal unit for survival. Big enough to produce two pairs. Small enough to move quickly. Fast enough to be able to get out of trouble if necessary and large enough to be able to deal with most situations.

The edge of the world was a tough place. Only the tough survived long there. The tribe Pugna, Obeo, Hiemo and Fugae came from was the toughest. The troupe had simple orders: scout the territory, find new hunting grounds, make sure they are secure.

For as long as anyone could remember this is what the tribe did. It established its territory. It defended it. Incrementally it got more territory. It defended that. It was not a strategy of great growth. It was a carefully planned approach that preserved the tribe's resources. More territory meant more people needed to defend it. More territory meant the tribe might attract more enemies. The tribe only got more territory when it felt it was strong enough to do so.

"This is how we survive." The Elders frequently said. "We plan our growth. We move only when we have the fighting men to defend new territory."

That was the first Rule. The Directive carved upon the tribe Commands Totem.

SONS BEGET TERRITORY. THROUGH SONS WE GROW

It was the first thing everyone saw when gazing upon it during Tribal Time when the tribe bonded over its shared history and accumulated wisdom. The lessons graven upon the Commands Totem were important to them. Young men, not yet warriors, gazed upon them and felt they understood where they were and what they were supposed to do. Older men, grizzled by the years, looked upon them and got a sense of the tribe's strength, a meaning of the passage of the years and the waning of their own strength.

The carvings on the Commands Totem were the distilled knowledge of the years. They, like everything else, helped the tribe survive. The Elders who ruled the tribe considered the Commands Totem to be their instrument. A visible expression not just of their authority but of the tribe's system of governance. They had, over the years, taken everything that happened to the tribe and everything the tribe did and analyzed it and boiled it down to nine key commands. These commands had become the heart of the tribe. The way it led its existence, made decisions and conducted business with other tribes.

Because of the Commands Totem and its carvings there were no misunderstandings. Everyone knew where they stood. Everyone understood what was expected of them.

Now that far away from that Totem, Pugna raised his arm and with a simple gesture stopped the troupe. They had come to the end of their journey. In front of them stood a dense wall of trees. The tribe's lands had shrubs and grass, but few trees. The rough, flat terrain made hunting a skill that required patience and the ability to use camouflage, speed and dexterity with a large number of hunting weapons.

The tribe's sons were amongst the best hunters in the world. Surviving in an inhospitable terrain that made hunting difficult they were also great fighters. Fierce, independent, capable of improvising on the spot. Hunting was an activity that made them feel alive: strong, powerful, one with nature, masters of their world.

The steppes and grasslands they hunted in, however were very different to the territory they were in right now. Pugna stood still, carefully surveying the thick wall of trees that rose before him. It would make visibility difficult, he thought. When you can't see what's round a bend in a path until you are practically upon it, it must be hard to react.

He suspected that the trees would make it easy for game to escape. The animals could weave in and out of the trunks of the great trees, some would probably climb up high on the trees themselves and disappear in the forest canopy overhead. He knew that the change in terrain negated many of his troupe's strengths and made them all weak, even vulnerable.

Change always works against us, he thought. It would have been great if the steppes could go on forever and ever, stretching from one edge of the world to the other. Then the tribe would simply expand, slowly and methodically. It would use its strength to incrementally gain and defend territory and anyone it did not beat it would simply turn into satellite tribes, paying fealty to it. This talk had been had more than once around the camp fires, late at night. This wall of trees was a problem. Pugna thought he could try to find a way around it, see just how big this forest was, but it would take time. Time he wasn't sure they had. His troupe had been sent on this because they were fast.

Going through them though constituted a risk. He thought carefully about that, weighing the odds. Leaders had to make choices. This was the second command on the tribe's Commands Totem. A troupe had a leader for a reason.

LEADERS ARE OUR STRENGTH

Leaders were the ones who made the decision, pointed the way, set the direction. When you lead, you were always under pressure. "We are going to enter the forest," Pugna said to his troupe. "Everything we encounter there is a potential threat to us." He watched their faces as the implications of his words sunk in. "We need to be on our guard."

The troupe understood that once they entered the forest many of their natural advantages would be lost. They would have to rely on each other even more, hoping that by staying alert together they would be able to see any threat long before it became a danger to them.

Silently, as one, the four men entered the forest. The world of the trees they entered was nothing like the steppes they'd left behind. The light inside the forest was different. Filtered through the canopy of leaves high overhead it was way darker and almost tinged with streaks of yellow. There were deep shadows here and patches of bright sunlight where there was the odd break in the canopy, high above their heads.

There appeared to be paths through the forest but where each led and what really lay ahead was hidden from them. The trunks of the massive trees around them hid the paths' end, made it difficult to decide which direction to take. From where he stood Pugna thought that one direction looked as good as another. How can leaders lead when there is no clear visibility to the paths they choose, thought Pugna.

It was not a thought he had the answer to. On the steppes you saw all paths. You made your decision based upon knowledge you possessed and the objectives you set. The third command on the tribe's Commands Totem made that clear:

LEADERS WEIGH ALL PATHS AVAILABLE

But here you had to make decisions based upon the unknowable. He was stuck. A good leader ought to be able to make good decisions. Decisions are based on knowing where to go. When you cannot know, how can you be a good leader? Pugna held the thought in his mind, knowing that the others were waiting for him to tell them what to do.

"We go this way," he said and pointed towards one of the paths opening up in front of them. When you do not know anything all paths are equally probable, he thought to himself.

In their new environment they made their way through the trees, carefully checking where they walked, their eyes and ears alert for any signs of danger. The path was narrow, thick vegetation rose on either side and they traveled in single file: Pugna, in front. Obeo, next behind him. Hiemo, next and finally Fugae, bringing up the rear.

They went on like this for more than an hour until they came upon a clearing. There were trees and vegetation, again on the other side. More paths to choose from. Pugna was busy thinking about how far they had traveled and whether the path he'd chosen had been a good one and he almost missed it, but Obeo, standing next to him didn't.

"People!" he hissed and because they had been bred and raised to hunt in the steppes where your prey is swift and success in the hunt demands cooperation, the troupe moved like one. They flattened themselves to the ground, removing themselves from view. Then, completely hidden for the moment they inched slowly forward, hiding behind the tall blades of grass in front of them.

Obeo had been right. On the other side of the clearing there was indeed, movement. The vegetation, between the trees was rustling and all of them could clearly see the points of spears like their own, held aloft, peering above it.

Presently there was a little more movement and the barely visible outline of a person wearing a massive headdress appeared, half-hidden behind one of the large tree trunks.

"Who goes there?" The person said. There was what appeared to be more movement in the trees behind him.

Pugna and his men froze. It may well be that they had not been seen. That the people across the clearing were only testing to see if anyone was around. He motioned with one hand for total silence.

Chapter 2

Perception

The world is not what it is. It is what we think it is. Every warrior of the tribe learnt this lesson the hard way. Combat presented a fluid situation. There were too many variables in the dynamic to make accurate predictions. Unexpected conditions could conspire to overturn an expected outcome. Tiny mistakes could lead to bigger ones, overturn expectations. The best warriors could be bested if they failed to believe in themselves. But self-belief and confidence always present a problem. Fail to take into account your opponent and self-belief in itself will not save you.

The thoughts we have are only the beginning. The combat ground is a testing ground. What we know has to change when the situation requires it. Nothing is ever left to blind chance.

These were hard lessons driven home by one unarmed combat match after another. And then learnt again by the mock battles the tribe's warriors routinely engaged in. Pitting one group against another. Evenly matched adversaries in terms of strength and speed and skill. Winners had to be smarter not just fitter.

Pugna was the product of this approach. They all were. In a group were they were all excellent fighters he got to lead because of his tactical brilliance. The same brilliance that was now being put to work as they all lay immobile amongst the trees, hidden by tall blades of grass, looking across the forest clearing and the place the voice had come from. There were obvious choices laid out before him. Pugna weighed each one with care.

He could remain quiet. The men on the other side would then come out of the clearing and Pugna and his troop would have the element of surprise. The things is there was no telling just how many men were on the other side of the clearing. There could be a lot more than they could fight off. There may be others nearby. These could be just the tip of a larger force. The uncertainties here were too great to leave to chance.

He looked at his men lying in the grass with him.

We could run, suggested Fugae. They have not seen us. We could go back to the village. Return with a much larger force.

Or we could just face them down, suggested Obeo. They don't know how many we are. We could feign we're a much larger force ourselves.

Hiemo kept quiet. Waiting until Pugna's gaze fell upon him. Wait it out, he said. If we stay here, quietly, we will see exactly how many there are and what they are like and we can decide then.

These were all credible choices, thought Pugna. Each made sense. Only one though was the best one. He went about assessing them the way he went about assessing anything: by weighing the risks. They were there because the tribe needed new territory. They needed to expand and had to scout. To go back and come back with a larger force of fighting men as Fugae had suggested, would waste time, allow the people on the other side of the clearing to do whatever they wanted. By the time the larger force had come back the situation would have changed and what, Pugna, thought if the people on the other side were also scouts? What if by the time a larger force came back they had gone? What then?

It was a waste of energy and resources that solved nothing and moved nothing forward. He discarded the option as non-viable.

There were more choices beyond fighting. The world is not what it is. It is what we think it is. What I think it now is what it will be, thought Pugna. He knew he was right in the sense that his actions would determine the outcome by precipitating the fluidity of the situation. In that sense every action would be right, but that was philosophical. Pugna had been tasked to get results. Outcomes determined real values: who lived, who died. What resources became available for the rest.

His mind made up he turned to his troupe. "Here are the choices," he said, explaining his reasoning for them all to understand. "We can fight, but we have no idea how many there are, or what they want."

"They want to kill us. They're armed." said Fugae, ignoring the fact that not to be armed in these parts was madness.

Pugna ignored the interruption, continued: "We can run, but then things will be unchallenged. We will have gained nothing, our mission will be lost and we will lose precious time." Everything else was a combination of these two. He took them through the odds. Watched them nervously fidget.

"There is something else we can do." He said, "as risky as everything else but with a higher possibility of success."

He carefully explained his plan to them. They would establish contact with the people on the other side without revealing themselves. If anything, they would work to create the impression that they were way more than four and much better armed. They would need to establish who the men on the other side were, how many. What they wanted. Once they had all the information they needed they would then make a better decision.

If things did not work out then Fugae and Obeo would have to run back. Go to the tribe. Get assistance. Pugna and Hiemo would stay behind. Run a diversion. Hold the attackers back as long as possible. Buy some time. If they could, then they too would run back. If not. Well. Everyone knew scouting was a risky business.

"It's really risky," Fugae volunteered at last. "What if we're injured? What if they are so many they can overrun us quickly?"

"We will give nothing away," said Pugna. "If they're not sure how many we are or even where we are exactly, they will find it hard to attack with accuracy which means they are unlikely to decide to do so. If things go wrong we only need to buy a little time. That we can do."

They all fell quiet after that. Each one contemplating the role they would have to play in the coming scenario. Intuitively they understood that Pugna's move was the best choice available to them. Tactically it decreased the risks and increased the potential of a positive outcome, even if things went wrong. They knew, as a leader, he was chosen, exactly for this kind of thinking.

They all knew what the Command Totem said:

LEADERS LEAD BY EXAMPLE.
NO LEADER ASKS MORE THAN HE IS PREPARED TO GIVE HIMSELF.

Pugna laid out the basic strategy for them. They would position themselves far enough apart to present a broad face to the men on the other side of the clearing. One that would make them appear like a much larger force. One of them would take all four spears, arrange them near him to make it look like there was a group of them on that side. The others would be responsible for generating telltale signs of a much bigger force. It may not work perfectly, Pugna thought, but it would create sufficient uncertainty to make the option of a fight, a difficult decision for the other side.

Once the plan was in motion they trusted each other to do their part. Pugna took the center of their layout. It gave him a better view of the clearing and, beyond it, the trees where the unknown enemy lay. We can only successfully pull this off if we work as one, he thought. The training of his men had been thorough. The daily contact and war games had taught each of them to focus on what they had to do, allow the others to do the same. In the tribe everyone carried their weight, did their job.

In this they were true professionals. The activity provided a relief from the pressure of having to workout the improbabilities of uncertain situations. They all concentrated on carrying out their tasks.

Pugna, in the meantime, kept a careful eye across the clearing, checking out the place from which the voice had come. They could, he reasoned, if they were really aggressive and really clever send part of their force to try and get around them, circumvent the clearing and sneak up on them from behind.

Logical as it was, right now that was the least likely option however. He knew that the other force did not yet know how many of them they were facing. To weaken themselves by splitting up like that was tactical suicide. It made it difficult for them to hold a frontal assault and made it even less likely of their flanking force surviving if they were, in turn, caught out or ambushed.

No, he thought. The other force is not moving a muscle until they truly know how many of us there are. It amazed him to see the pivotal role information played in a fight. After all, they trained all their lives to fight. Fighting is what kept the tribe strong, yet without information no warrior really wanted to fight if there was an alternative. There were just too many uncertainties.

Time seemed to slow down for them all. At one point Pugna saw a number of spears peak over the covering foliage on the other side of the clearing. Low-hanging tree branches rustled. The tall blades of grass seemed to stir.

"We know you're there." Came the voice again. As strong and confident as before. "Show yourselves!"

Pugna waited. His men were already in action. Obeo was already creating the impression on their flank of a large armed group. Fugae and Hiemo allowed themselves to appear careless. They moved grass leaves, touched branches themselves. From across the clearing the entire front facing them would appear to be coming to life, Pugna thought. Inwardly he smiled.

"Who are you?" he asked and immediately moved to get to another place. He was aware that giving away his position like this made him vulnerable. Made them all vulnerable by association. Carefully he peered across the clearing again.

Against the intense greenery of the backdrop he fancied he saw a plumed headdress for a moment. It then disappeared. "We are the tribe of the South. The tribe called Fortis." Said the voice. "We are here to explore, make the world larger."

Pugna had never heard of a tribe called Fortis but then again he was not one for tribal names. He did not go to trading posts much. Did not care for too much contact with outsiders. His main concern, always, was the quality of his tribe's fighting men. His own ability in the field.

"We mean you no harm." The voice continued. "Show yourselves and let us talk."

Pugna said nothing. His men continued their task, making it appear that they were a much larger force than they were. The fact that the strangers were so quick to talk, did not appear to change position after each exchange worried him. It was either a signal of strength on their part or inexperience. Either of these was dangerous: a strong opponent would eventually make their move, overwhelm them. An inexperienced one would make unexpected and probably irrational moves, precipitate their hand. Lead to an unwanted escalation.

He thought about both options, not entirely discarding the notion that there could also be that he was facing the volatile situation of a larger, more powerful and yet inexperienced force. The worst of all worlds. Life outside the tribe and its territories was never short of interesting, he thought.

He decided to probe them a little. "Show yourselves, first!" he yelled.

He counted the possibilities. If they did it would tell him a lot. He would be able to see them, weigh up who they were and what they wanted on a personal level. Right now all the information he had was impersonal. He knew the risks of that. They all did:

PEOPLE TRUMP INFORMATION
CONTEXT IS EVERYTHING

There was silence from the other side. Pugna thought that they would be weighing the options.

The day grew longer and no more words were exchanged between Pugna and his troupe and the unknown force of people on the other side of the clearing. But that did not mean things did not happen. As the day drew on and the sun moved across the sky Pugna noticed that there were more and more appearances of spear tips from the other side. Quietly he crawled to where Obeo was busy rearranging the spears, tips held aloft. He agreed with him to become a little more energetic, make it appear there were more than a group or two of them.

Similarly, Fugae and Hiemo stepped up their activity. The noise level from their side rose a notch. The side of the forest facing the clearing and the tribe called Fortis came to life. Rustlings, calls, the occasional noise of gear moving as wood struck wood, or a metal spear tip touched a tree. Many feet sounded to be marching.

There was a response from the other side. Pugna thought he heard voices. The branches rustled even more. He fancied he saw a headdress or two peer from across but in the falling gloom he could no longer be sure. At least we are engaging, he thought. Each response told him something he now needed to understand.

As darkness fell the noise level coming from the other side rose a little. Pugna found it a little astonishing until he recognized the sounds for what they were: fires being lit. Food being cooked. How many were there across the clearing he wondered again?

He couldn't risk their lighting fires in the forest. They were too few of them to keep an eye on them and should things go wrong the forest burning would not help them. He decided on a different strategy, however. He instructed Obeo and Fugae to cut down suitable branches, find out hollowed out trunks. The noise they made was sufficient to make it sound like there were at least a score of them, maybe more.

Once they had found what he asked them each had an improvised drum. The hollowed out trunks they used made a deep, resonant sound when struck. Every member of the tribe was versed in the language of the drums. All through the night, while their possible opponents cooked food and ate and drunk, Pugna and his men made sure their drums never slept.

If we keep them awake they will feel the pressure, he reasoned. It did mean that he and his men would also end up staying up all night, but the tribe's people were used to that too. No hardship was enough to deter them from anything. Functioning while being sleep deprived was something they learnt while very young.

Boom! Boom! Boom! Boom! Went the language of the drums, putting sounds in groups together and splitting them apart.

We are the tribe of the North. The drums said, *we nor fear nor run from war. We are the tribe of the North. We are them men who win wars.*

The message was repeated on and on and on. Pugna knew that the rhythm was known. Even if no one could put a name to their tribe that drum call came every time their tribe won a mock battle, every time their tribe was in a competitive engagement. The drum call was part of their reputation, the thing that made them stand out from anyone. They played it in advance as they approached a trading outpost or a village. And they played it every time they were victorious, and their tribe was victorious often.

Their tribe had a reputation and Pugna was now calling it in.

Steady and unwavering their drummed message played throughout the night. They deliberately changed logs after a while, each of them getting to use a slightly different drum, make a slightly different sound. As the sound traveled upwards it bounced off and through branches and foliage, was added to by the rustle of leaves and the flutter of feathers until, from the side of the forest of the tribe called Fortis looking across the clearing in a darkness broken only by the glow from campfires and the odd firefly it really seemed as if the whole jungle was alive and a small army was hiding, waiting for them, there.

Meanwhile, on Pugna's side of the forest a strange thing was happening. Pugna, Fugae, Obeo and Hiemo beat lustily upon their makeshift drums. Arms conditioned by fighting banged away all night. They swapped drums and drummed and drummed and smiled crazily in the dark until the sleeplessness and the banging and the tension of the day melded into something else.

We are invincible. They would drum from time to time along with their message to the tribe across the clearing. *We never falter.* And because they were tired and sleepless and yet drummed on, the words made them smile crazily. They would catch each other's eyes glinting in the dark and they would nod and their lips would pull back exposing wide smiles until in their minds the fear and the uncertainty began to melt away.

This was their element. They had been trained to fight from birth and intimidation was a game they knew how to play well. The long hours stopped being their concern and fatigue in their arms stopped being an issue.

When the first light broke and the darkness of the forest melted into gray shadows they looked at each other, seeing dark hollowed out eyes, skin gray from fatigue, glistening with sweat. It was the determination inside them however that suddenly made them special. Their eyes, deep inside their sockets now all told the same story.

They were prepared to make a stand. Stop the people from across the clearing, make them pay dearly for each step they took. The passage of the night had forced them to strip away everything but what they were really good at and though the task might really be impossible, the situation truly hopeless, they were now ready to face their enemy and die if necessary

Chapter 3

Assessment

So morning came. The drumming from Pugna's troupe stopped. There was no noise from the Fortis tribe either. Each side, sleepless and stressed found itself struggling to take stock of the situation.

Pugna looked at his men and recognized the determination in them. He knew well enough himself the effect that such intense drumming and tension had. He could feel the grim determination to fight in himself. The relief that came when a decision had been made and he was alert of the pitfalls this approach presented.

There was a line on the Command Totem that warned:

CHOICES PROVIDE CLARITY
CHOOSE WISELY

Choices made under forced conditions were rarely wise. In the cold light of day he knew he had to assess things better. As the leader of the troupe he knew he could not afford himself the luxury of losing himself in the heat of the moment. The previous day had been led by perceptions.

The tribe called Fortis was there with more men than his, of that he was now certain and they were all armed with spears. But that did not necessarily mean that their intentions were bad. He knew that the show he and his man had put on through the night made them look every bit as dangerous and hostile as they thought the Fortis people were.

Our fears fill the gaps left by the absence of real information. That had been an early lesson for him as a fighter. He said it inside his head a few times now, as a personal mantra, hearing the words and trying to feel their wisdom. A larger number of the enemy did not scare him. If anything that was a weakness in itself. In these woods numbers did not give an immediate advantage, he and his men could manoeuvre deftly amongst the trees, pick them off one by one before they could bring the weight of their numbers to bear.

A sleepless, tired enemy was always low on morale. Pugna knew that too. He and his men were hardened to lack of sleep. They had been trained from a young age to do more with less and that included everything (food, supplies, rest). They were now in their element. Each passing hour that made fatigue heavier on minds and bodies that had not slept a wink through the night equalized the playing field, made Pugna's troupe stronger.

"I don't think they liked our drumming much," said Obeo. He stood next to Pugna looking across the clearing the Fortis tribe appeared indeed to be in some disarray. In the strengthening light they caught a first glimpse of people who seemed to be leaning on their spears for support.

"The day's young," Pugna said. He looked at the rest of the members of his small troupe, painfully aware of the impossible task that lay ahead of them. "They will soon recover and think a little more clearly."

"Let's rattle them some more. Stop them from recovering," Obeo's voice was clearly excited. The other members of the troupe nodded energetically, they were all in agreement, eager to press their advantage home. Pugna thought how easy it is to let events guide you. You do something. The other side does something else. You do something next. Things tend to take a course all of their own.

He also knew that true warriors never let circumstances control them. So far they had been operating on assumptions. Assumptions drawn from the few facts they had:

- There was another tribe in the area
- That tribe, called Fortis, was armed
- The force they were facing was greater than their own

That was all. From those three facts had sprung an entire scenario that had necessitated their drumming wildly through the night, telling the Fortis tribe what badass warriors they were and how they were eager to get the tips of their spears tinted red. And now, here they all were. His troupe caught up in the spirit of the moment trying to think of ways to escalate things even further. The other side, now possibly convinced that it was dealing with a force of homicidal maniacs at least as large as their own.

Great. We have a stalemate of sorts.

Pugna told himself that the drumming through the night, had been necessary. His small force had to somehow change the balance of power.

ASYMMETRICAL RELATIONSHIPS NEVER WORK

This was a line on the Commands Totem that every troupe leader had to ponder. Whatever their intentions if the Fortis people did not take them seriously there would be unnecessary and probably avoidable violence.

If they tried to attack them, they would have fought back, ferociously. But suppose for a moment they didn't, Pugna thought to himself. Suppose they were as peaceful as they said they were and simply came over and laid claim to the rest of the forest. Again, if they'd failed to take Pugna's troupe seriously, the dismissal would cause issues that would result in bloodshed.

In fact, bloodshed seemed to be the outcome of most moves Pugna could think of. Except the current one. Here they were locked in uncertain mental combat. Two sides, neither willing just yet to break the impasses and attack, though Pugna thought, his troupe had to be held back if anything, by his presence.

"We could split up now," Fugae suggested. "Obeo and I could flank them, start picking them off."

Inaction now was as dangerous as the wrong kind of action. Pugna knew that too. The Fortis tribe might be potentially hostile. If they sat on their hands and did nothing the only thing that was guaranteed to happen was that in their imagination the Fortis tribe would grow in threat until they were all baby-killing monsters that had to be eradicated from the face of the Earth.

We need better information, thought Pugna. Without information our decisions are flawed. We are thinking blind. It was a Northern tribe expression. To think you needed to see with your mind, not your eyes.

"You," he pointed at Fugae. "I want you to try and get round to their far flank," he pointed towards the general direction of the Fortis tribe. "Don't engage any of them. Be invisible," he admonished. "I just want you to come back and tell us what you saw."

Fugae nodded to show he understood. He picked up his spear and left, his form moving silently, like a shadow in the forest.

"You," Pugna pointed at Hiemo. "You do the same. The other flank. See how far this clearing goes." Hiemo nodded quietly. He too picked up his spear and disappeared into the forest.

That left only Pugna and Obeo. "I want you to get a little to the left of me from here," Pugna said. "Find a tall tree and climb up. See what you can spot from there."

Obeo nodded his ascent. He left his spear behind. Climbing a tree was hard enough without needing to carry a spear. Besides, he was not going to be too far away from Pugna.

Left on his own Pugna got down on the tall grass and inch by inch slithered towards the edge of the clearing. Without being seen he peered across at where he knew the Fortis tribe people were. He waited a decent while carefully observing, waiting for his men to get into position. Then, when he was almost certain that they had each, by now, reached the part of the forest where they should be he played his hand.

"You there!" he yelled across the clearing at the Fortis tribe people.

He waited while the sound of his voice carried across. There was some time before anything happened. Pugna fancied he could discern some kind of activity. The background noise level went up from the other camp.

"You there!" he repeated after a decent while. Getting no reply he asked: "What is it you want here?"

There was silence. Eventually a head poked above the greenery at the other end. Pugna remained in hiding as he studied it. It belonged to a man in a fancy headdress. Eyes big and outlined in black charcoal. War stripes painted on it. "We are exploring the forest." He said. He waited for Pugna to reply (which he didn't). The silence weighed on him. His eyes darted around trying to spot Pugna's hiding place. When that failed he said at last: "We come in peace. We really mean no harm." He waited some more and getting no further reply, he disappeared behind the tall grasses again.

Pugna thought it was interesting. He waited for the others to get back before he developed his own thoughts, further.

Sure enough, an hour later all three of his men came back. From the vantage point each had chosen they'd had a clearer view of the enemy camp and were now ready to report back on their observations.

Fugae started first. He'd managed to get to the edge of the clearing, go round it and then he'd crawled on his belly for ages until he got to the perimeter of the enemy camp. He was hidden in deep bushes, unable to move or make a sound, his eyes seeing things through the few cracks that the dense foliage permitted.

"There are many of them," he began. "I counted many feet. They wear anklets of sharpened teeth and from what I saw have spears they lean on as they walk. I saw one of them close up. His toes were black. There were strange markings on his ankle."

"I saw strange markings too," said Hiemo. He too had managed to skirt the clearing on the other side of the enemy camp. He was hiding in a clump of bushes, unable to move a muscle should he give himself away while he observed. A handy opening in the bushes provided him with glimpses of the Fortis tribesmen as they went around their business. "They have markings on their chests," he said, "some have the symbol of some tortoise and some have an eagle," he said. "They believe in animal magic," he concluded. "When you started calling out they ran around, they were very agitated."

But it was Obeo who had the best quality information of all. Perched high above the forest floor, he'd managed to get a clear view of the enemy camp. "There are a score of them at least," he said. "They all have spears and carry knives in their belts. When you called out they panicked for some reason. They ran around until they found a man with a massive headdress. It was he who came out to speak to you. When you did not reply he ran back to a part of the forest which is obscured by branches. I could not see what he did there or if he spoke to anyone."

Pugna considered carefully what each of them said. "What do you think?" he asked, finally.

"They are monsters, not like us," opined Himeo. "I say we send one of us back, get reinforcements, while the rest of us keep these intruders at bay."

Pugna nodded at his words. "And you?" he asked Fugae.

"I agree," Fugae said. "I did not see their faces, but by their feet I know they're not like us. They're vile beings who will want to attack us. I say we attack them first."

Pugna also nodded his head at Fugae's words.

Finally it was Obeo's turn to speak. "There are too many of them and too few of us. In the trees, here, perhaps we can hold them back, maybe even defeat them. In the open they will use their numbers. We cannot hope to fight them like that."

"Seems like we have few choices that do not lead to us fighting them," said Pugna speaking to all his men.

"If we surprise them we can defeat them, of that I am sure," said Obeo.

Pugna had to agree. By the account of his men he could see that the sleeplessness and fatigue were taking their toll. The Fortis tribe might be more numerous in their numbers but they were not hardier. Their resolve was suffering, their efficiency was being weakened.

They'd failed to attack or even send out any scouts and despite the fact that they'd answered his call, they had been discomfited by his subsequent silence. He carefully weighed everything he now knew about them and he could see that the longer they waited the stronger they became and the weaker the enemy was.

There was a definite symmetry of power being established in the relationship but he was concerned, right now on just how they could cement that.

"Do you think they know how strong we are?" he asked his troupe. He watched them all nod vehemently. As a leader he knew that what was important was that his decisions reflected the reality of what he saw instead of what his men expected of him. It was a fine line of distinction that was based on clear thinking.

"At least we know what they want," Obeo said. "They are explorers, just like us."

Later that night, as darkness once again started to fall across the forest Pugna found himself, once more, alone, peering across the clearing towards where the Fortis tribe was also getting ready to face the night.

Reasoning told him that when two groups of people wanted the same thing only one could get it. Did that make a battle inevitable? He wondered about it a little. When it was a matter of life and death the choices were clear. The action was guided by the imperatives of the moment where you could not afford to lose. This, he admitted to himself, was a little different. Amongst his troupe he was the only one who could see it.

The forest is large. It should be big enough for two tribes. The thought was a revelation to him. Traditionally tribes did not work together. They did not stay too close to each other. That was tempting fate. Soon, what one tribe had another tribe would covet and you'd have to prove you were strong enough to keep it.

He knew that part of his tribe's strength was its isolation. Anyone entering into their lands was an enemy. They dealt with enemies severely.

Now, of course, they were outside the tribal lands. But so was the Fortis tribe. It was a new situation where they were meeting on ground that did not belong to either. The rules of engagement here were uncertain.

What if I start a war? He thought. Then again he knew the answer to that. To start a war there had to be survivors who would take news of their attack and defeat back to the Fortis tribe village. If the enemy was totally annihilated there would be no war. Just another victory for his men.

We could attack under cover of darkness, he thought. They will be too tired and too deeply asleep to realize what is happening until it's too late. The prospect of overcoming this many enemies and winning a great victory was not unattractive. The name of Pugna and his men would be sung in the tribe songs, around camp fires for a very long time.

Or, he thought, we could wait it out a little longer. Weaken them some more, see what happens. Sometimes, he knew, events had a way of working themselves out. Circumstances precipitating outcomes. That thought too was not without its attraction. It held few direct risks and as the troupe with the fewest number of warriors, holding back a superior force they would be deemed to be heroes, anyway.

Then maybe what's required is that we call for reinforcements. That was the logical thing to do. The tribe however had tasked them to gain more land. The Fortis tribe right now was an obstacle, not a threat. He considered carefully everything he'd found out about them.

As he was thinking all this he saw the tall grass across the clearing move unnaturally in the falling gloom. Then, almost like magic, out of it rose the same man in the tall headdress that Pugna had seen earlier that day. The man, had his spear with him. He stood, in the open. Body flexed for rapid movement. For long moments nothing happened. He stood there, feet firmly planted apart. Spear in one hand. Eyes fixed towards where Pugna was, though Pugna knew well that he had not been seen.

Then, as Pugna watched, the man hefted his spear, weighed it carefully over his right shoulder, judging the distance with his heft the way only an expert spear-thrower could. Then with a mighty throw he sent is sailing across the clearing, making it to a tree on the left of Pugna, where the spear embedded itself with a thud. Its sharp tip buried deep in the tree trunk, its haft quivering.

Pugna, moved with trained speed. He slithered back a little, making sure he remained out of sight still. Then he stood up. Took careful aim with his own spear and with all his strength threw it across the clearing himself. Next to the figure that had thrown his so defiantly was a smaller tree. Its trunk a few feet behind the man. Pugna's spear flew true and it flew fast. It whistled past the man standing there, its passage making the plumes on his headdress quaver and its tip, struck the tree trunk and bit deep into it. Its thud was deep, strong. A clear message in itself.

When Pugna looked again the men in the headdress had vanished, his form melted back behind the trees. All that was left of the silent exchange between them were two spears, their tips buried deep in opposite tree trunks across a clearing in a forest no one had named or claimed just yet.

"Obeo, Hiemo," Pugna commanded as he got back to his troupe. "Get the drums ready, we have a long night ahead of us."

An exchange of spears

Chapter 4

Connection

The night that passed was hard on all of them. Pugna and his men took turns this time, grabbing a little sleep in small chunks, maintaining their alertness just as they maintained the psychological pressure on the Fortis tribe, across the clearing.

This time we shall finally have a reckoning Obeo thought to himself as he drummed through the night. It was a thought he shared with Hiemo who nodded in agreement and Fugae until the three of them were so convinced that this was what Pugna was planning that they were barely able to sleep a little when their time came to do so.

Like every fighting member of the tribe they had been taught to fight for what they wanted and what they wanted was always worth fighting for. The entire troupe knew the rules it lived by:

If you want something – get it
If it's someone else's and you need it – take it
If it's yours or the tribe's – defend it

Within the tribe itself there was a culture of help, cooperation and where possible, sharing.

THE TRIBE IS YOUR FAMILY

It was a simple enough rule that allowed the tribe to focus on survival without having to worry about conflict within its ranks.

The sun rising over the forest found them all with the knowledge that this was a critical day. Pugna's troupe understood that if they continued what they were doing eventually the sleeplessness and the fatigue would wear them down too.

"Do you think they've gone away?" Fugae said. "They're awfully quiet and I can't smell any campfire."

It was true. As the sun rose and the light got stronger the forest was unusually quiet. Pugna who had not slept a wink all night picked himself up from where he had lain, watching the clearing. His eyes were still on the spear he'd thrown, stuck fast in the tree. He had left the spear that had been thrown intact, too.

We're connected by our spears. The thought had been with him all night, niggling at the edges of his mind. He'd crafted his spear with care. Had carefully selected the hardwood of his haft and he had made sure the metal point had been sharpened to a razor edge. Pugna had spent a lifetime practicing his throwing until he felt he could guide a spear with his mind's eye directly to the target.

The night before, the action by the man in the headdress had taken him by surprise. Caught him unprepared. He'd never thought that they'd be exchanging spears like that. When he'd thrown his back in retaliation he'd seen in his mind, clearly where the man stood. Where the tree behind him was. He'd thrown his spear without thinking too deeply. Its target had never been intended to be the man. Just the tree.

Why? He asked that of himself now. The natural response would have been to assume the man was a threat. He'd just thrown a spear at him (well, at the tree next to him) and remove him. Pugna was a seasoned fighter who put great store by his instincts.

The thought of the thrown spear was tormenting him.

"What's the plan? How do we attack?" Hiemo asked the moment he saw Pugna. There was an eagerness in Hiemo's face that made Pugna realize just how much his men hated the uncertainty of inaction, the indecisions that went with waiting. They were warriors, at their best when the action called them to do what they did best.

He understood that action required clear directions. Left little room for the fog of confusion. But the wrong kind of action created legacies, started off feuds that went on for years. "Stay here," he told his men. "Do nothing."

He went back to the place where he'd spent the night. Being cautious he made his way carefully, on his stomach, trying to keep the grass around him from moving and giving away his presence. His lying immobile, all night, had flattened the grass and created a natural receptacle for him. It lay there, waiting, like a cradle and his body naturally fit into it as he slowly crawled in.

Gently, with one hand, he parted the tall blades of grass rising in front of him. He peered across the clearing. The tree where he had thrown his spear stood there. The spear was gone. He looked at it, wanting to make sure. He knew that the spear, his spear had been there at first light. He had seen it and at one stage, in the very early hours of the morning he had even entertained the crazy thought of running across, grabbing it and returning with it.

It would have been suicide and he'd obviously abandoned the idea for what it was: the craziness of a brain waking up in the early morning, after a second night without sleep. Now the spear was gone. Someone had taken it.

He looked to his left where the spear that had been thrown at him had struck the tree and that was still there. No one had touched it.

Puzzled by what was happening and yet unable to completely understand it Pugna wormed his way to the tree trunk and took careful cover behind it. Slowly he stood up, still completely covered by it. He knew that if he reached out with his hand and grabbed the spear and attempted to pull it out he wouldn't be able to. It was too deeply embedded in the tree. His position from behind the tree trunk did not give him enough leverage.

No, in order to pull the spear out of the tree he'd have to take a quick step around it. Exposing himself. He'd then be able to grab it and pull it out. But could he do it quickly enough that he didn't get picked off by the enemy?

Suppose there were three, four spear throwers at the other side, patiently waiting for him to do just this. Would they not then be able to get a bead on his position and pick him off? One spear he could perhaps avoid, but three or more he couldn't. One was simply bound to get him.

He could, of course, choose to just leave the spear where it was. Get back to his men and see if he could form a plan of attack. Except his own spear had gone. Someone had been crazy enough to do just what Pugna was thinking he shouldn't.

Either the Fortis tribesmen were much, much braver than he gave them credit for or they were not worried about sacrificing one of their number. Or maybe they were just simply crazy, too little sleep and too much fear had suddenly combined to make them lose all inhibitions. Pugna had seen that before. He'd seen people go into battle screaming at the top of their voices, their eyes glazed with that special mental fog that mental and physical exhaustion bring about. They'd been easy pickings.

Speculation, of course, was not going to solve his problem. There was just one way to find out. Taking a deep breath, and knowing he was now taking a calculated risk, Pugna quickly stepped around the tree trunk, exposed his flank to the side of the clearing where the Fortis tribe was. He reached up quickly with one hand, grabbed the haft of the spear, pulled it out of the tree trunk with one, quick move.

He kept half an eye at the clearing, fully expecting to see the blurred movement of thrown spears. Certain death flying his way.

Nothing.

He waited a second longer looking directly at the clearing now, turning to face it full on.

Still nothing. Not a sound. Not a single movement. Pugna looked at the spear he was holding, weighed it in his hand. He then turned round and holding the spear, melted back into the forest.

Obeo, Fugae and Hiemo found him an hour later, sitting with his back to a tree, quietly facing towards the clearing, about 50 meters away from him and hidden from view by the tall grass. He was holding the spear in both hands. Looking at the intricate pattern on it. Checking out its weight and feel.

"Where have you been?" they asked almost with one voice. They looked at the spear he held.

"What's that?" Obeo asked first.

"It's the spear of their chief. The man in the headdress," said Pugna.

"How did you get it?"

"He threw it at a tree near me. Yesterday," said Pugna, choosing carefully each word to describe exactly what had happened.

"What? We should have attacked then. They've started war," Obeo's reaction was predictable.

"We don't defend trees," Pugna said.

"They attacked!" countered Obeo.

"No, he aimed at the tree."

"How do you know?"

"Look," said Pugna holding the spear aloft for them to see. "What do you see?"

They all peered at it carefully. The spear's haft was of polished wood. It was brown with a careful lacquer that had been applied to it. It shone as the light caught it. The spear had been carefully weighed. The middle of it where the balance point was, was marked by carefully threaded cured leather straps. They wound around the wood tightly. Sealed with expert tying that hid the edges.

The spear could be gripped and wielded without it slipping out of your grasp. The point of it was of bright metal. The tip, straight and round was designed to go deep into whatever it was aimed at. Unlike the spears of the tribe that were triangular at the tip, meant to inflict as much damage as possible when thrown, this one was round and pointy. Meant for penetrating at depth.

"Their spears are lighter than ours," Hiemo spoke first, guessing correctly. "They have to rely on speed to get penetration. We can do way more damage."

"They polish the wood of their weapons," Fugae spoke up. "They don't do hand to hand combat with them. Polished wood is slippery."

"The spear tapers at both ends," said Obeo who was an expert on these things. "They can be thrown far if you have a strong arm."

They made a few more suggestions analyzing the technical characteristics of the weapon and comparing to their own, heavy spears. Theirs were implements of war designed to bring down whatever they hit. Pugna listened to them quietly until at last he said: "Look again, do you see anything else?"

They looked perplexed at him and then at the weapon. Then back at him.

"Look at the haft," he suggested.

They had but without focusing exclusively upon it. Now, directed by their leader to look at it Pugna's men focused on the haft of the spear. Beneath the lacquered surface were designs. Intricately carved and painted scenes of animals. Groups of people walking with them, huts and children playing amongst them.

Their eyes slowly followed the painstaking drawings, etched on the wood and painted before being sealed by the lacquer. The artist who had done this had taken long months, maybe even years to complete it. The haft told a tale. One of a tribe with children and men and women, living somewhere where they had animals and water and plenty of food.

The scenes unfolding were peaceful, serene even. Paradoxically given the medium upon which they had been carved, there was not a single weapon in sight in the pictures.

"What is that?" Fugae asked first.

"It's their village. Where they come from," said Pugna.

Compared to the spears they had that had no marking upon them the spear Pugna held in his hands was a work of art. "Why would someone go into all this trouble to create a spear that will be lost in a battle?" Obeo asked.

"Why indeed," said Pugna, passing the spear to him. Obeo took it, hefted it feeling its weight. Carefully peered at the scenes engraved in the haft. The others clustered around him. "Maybe, they don't use it as a weapon," Hiemo contributed. "Maybe they use it only for ceremonies."

The point of the spear looked worn. Its edge sharp. They tested it by pressing a thumb upon it. It broke the skin at the slightest pressure.

They spent some time looking at the weapon, trying to understand what it was that Pugna had. In the meantime Pugna was thinking. *We're connected by our spears. Our weapons define us.*

It was true.

The revelation changed for him the way he interpreted everything he knew about the Fortis tribe. Although he could not completely articulate what it was he felt inside him, he understood now what it was he had to do.

"This is the plan," he said to his companions and they looked up, all hopeful.

Sometime later, he stood at the edge of the clearing where he'd been hiding by the tree at which the spear had been thrown. He was in clear view of the Fortis tribe, he knew. "You there!" he called out to them.

"What do you want?" he was answered quickly.

Pugna picked his next sentence carefully. "I think we need to talk. Face to face. No tricks," he said.

There was silence.

"We do not need to fight." Pugna yelled.

"How do we know you're not tricking us?"

Pugna smiled to himself at this. At least they were thinking about it. Asking straight questions, which meant they wanted straight answers.

My spear for theirs. It didn't get any straighter than that except the spear he'd thrown at them did not tell the whole story. It only said that the tribe he'd come from were proficient at killing. War was their game. There was more to them than war. *But our spears don't show that.*

"We both want the same thing," Pugna said.

Silence. Then: "What?"

"Sons."

Before they got to this point Pugna had explained his plan to his men.

"That's totally crazy," Obeo had said when he'd heard it. The others nodded vigorously in agreement, unable to believe their ears.

"This is what we will do, I will do," Pugna had explained, "I will go and talk to them. Unarmed. If they really are a threat they will try to kill me. They may succeed of course, but not before I have given a good account of myself. At any rate you will know what they really want. Fall back, get to the tribe. Come back with reinforcements. Kill them all. But if they really are looking for peace. If they really mean us no harm, then we will just talk."

"No one puts themselves in harm's way like this," Fugae said. "This is crazy,"

"Yes, maybe." I have seen their spears, Pugna thought. He felt a deep connection with the man who had thrown it. He'd chosen to reveal more than his words to Pugna. Pugna's spear, thrown in return did not tell the whole story. He knew he had to add to it.

So, now. As he stood at the very edge of the clearing, protected still by the trunk of a tree his men whispered to him that it was not too late. They could all still change the plan. Pugna silenced them with a curt motion of one palm.

"I am coming out. To talk," he said and with that he gingerly stepped round the tree trunk. He held his hands, palms open, at waist height to show that he was unarmed. "I have no weapons," he said, stressing every word.

And so unarmed, sleepless, tired. Pugna took a few more steps. He stood, alone and vulnerable in the very center of the clearing he had been ready to fight over. He looked across where the Fortis tribesmen lay hidden.

And there, he waited.

The Tribe's Commands Totem

Throughout his mission Pugna made choices guided by the accumulated wisdom of his tribe. Commands that were meant to help him survive.

SONS BEGET TERRITORIES
THROUGH SONS WE GROW

LEADERS ARE OUR STRENGTH

LEADERS WEIGH ALL PATHS AVAILABLE

LEADERS LEAD BY EXAMPLE
NO LEADER ASKS MORE THAN HE IS PREPARED TO DO

PEOPLE TRUMP INFORMATION

CONTEXT IS EVERYTHING

CHOICES PROVIDE CLARITY
CHOOSE WISELY

ASYMMETRICAL RELATIONSHIPS NEVER WORK

THE TRIBE IS YOUR FAMILY

With time, as the world changed the tribe added one more line to their Commands Totem:

RISKS MUST BALANCE REWARDS

How do these reflect your experience of the guidelines of your organization? Where is it better? Where is it worse? How would you improve on any of them? If this was your tribe would you be able to run it successfully based just on these? Give full reasons for your answers.

Epilogue

A hunter, somewhere in the Midwest, came upon a farmer. The hunter had been away a long time, chasing his quarry, hunting it down and killing it. He had accumulated cured meat and pelts. Sharpened bone needles and bone daggers. Ornaments from the teeth of many animals.

The farmer had a lot of work to do because it had been a good year and the harvest had been rich. He was out inspecting one of his fields when the hunter came into his land, his horse laden with the fruit of his labors trailing behind, the reins loosely held in one hand.

"I greet you," the farmer gave the customary greeting of the midlands.

"I greet you back," smiled the hunter and raised his empty right hand to show he meant no harm.

"The hunting was good," the farmer said looking at the heavily laden horse.

"Yes, much to take to the market. How was your harvest?"

They exchanged more pleasantries and news. The farmer told the hunter about the latest market fair and the expansion of one of the marketplaces that now bought grain on faith before it was produced. "If I make more than I told them I would, they buy the amounted they committed to at the price we agreed and I am free to sell the rest," explained the farmer. "If it is a bad year however and my crops fail I am in debt to them and it will take a lot of work to repair the damage done to my credit."

The hunter listened in wonder at this. It was astonishing that things could be bought and sold before they'd even been grown. He much preferred, he said, his own trade where the certainties were much greater.

"The problem is that there are just so many of us now." He explained how a tribe living at the very edge of the world had cornered the market in fighting and hunting skills. They'd come out of their isolation and had joined forces with another tribe he thought was called Fortis, but he could not be sure. Together the two tribes had grown in numbers and wealth.

"They sell their skills, teaching us." He explained how he, himself had spent a whole year living with them, learning about how to track game and throw a spear. How to fight bears and take down opponents. Then he'd learnt about calligraphy and the art of fine wood carving, components needed for keeping good records and also leaving notes behind, so that the parts of the world he passed through were marked with his passage and there were messages for others to find.

"The world is joining up fast," he concluded. "A hunter could go for months, maybe years without seeing another human being." Now, he'd seen a band of hunters not two days ago. A whole band of them!

"Yes, the days are changing," agreed the farmer.

Together the two men made their slow way to the farmstead. The hunter could stay for a few nights, the farmer said, in exchange for some pelts, maybe some trinkets for his daughters. The hunter agreed, added a few of his sharpest bone knives, in exchange for a bag of corn and some flour. He also said he wanted to know more about the marketplace nearby. The one where the farmer sold his harvest in advance.

"I will gladly tell you," the farmer said to him as they walked side by side. "I really need to hear about this tribe at the edge of the world. The services they offer. I have a son who doesn't like farming and to become a skilled hunter like you may just be the thing."

Activities

The Trust Workbook

Tribal Trust

In Pugna's tribe the rule of law came down through the Elders. They distilled it into a code of nine commands that created a framework everyone could work with. The commands acted as guidelines through which leaders could make better choices. A leader chosen to command could be trusted to understand the guidelines well enough to apply them to the parameters of the mission he was tasked with.

1. Explain how, in your organization, do you achieve the same thing?

2. Do you have the same sense of belonging to a tribe? What are the characteristics that make this happen? (Include items such as branding elements in your answer)

3. Do you trust the judgment of those who lead in your organization?

Throughout the story of the *Tribe That Discovered Trust*, Pugna made his thought processes transparent to his men, asking their opinion, involving them in the decision making process and explaining his plan and his thoughts to them.

1. Detail the processes that include you in the decision making process in your organization

2. Describe how communication takes place in your organization (top down, memos, meetings, formally/informally etc)

3. Now describe how that style of communication makes you feel (do you feel listened to? Included? Ignored?)

4. How do you decide when to trust those you work with? Detail your own thinking process

5. Explain what you do when you find yourself not trusting in the judgment of someone in a position of power in your organization but know that you still need to follow their directions

6. How do you think trust could be made easier to establish in your organization?

7. Describe the ideal set up that would make it easier for you to trust the people you work with. Also explain what should happen when trust is broken.

The story of *The Tribe That Discovered Trust* is split into four chapters, each of them represents a trust-building step.

Contact

In Chapter I – Contact is first made with the tribe called Fortis.

1. Does the immediate contact made live up to expectations in the context of what is happening in their world? If you've answered "yes", detail all the elements that you think actually add up to it and help it make sense. If you've answered "no" explain your reasons and give a breakdown of all the different elements that you think do not live up to expectation.

2. Detail what would happen if you have an initial contact with someone that defies everything you expect to see or hear. Would it help you build trust in them faster or slower? Explain the role played by context in your answer.

3. In Chapter I – Pugna recalls the three first Rules from his tribe's Commands Totem. Explain the significance or meaning of each one in the context of the story and then explain their meaning in terms of what you do in your organization: How does it grow? What are its limiting principles? What stops it from being bigger and more successful? How do leaders lead in it? How does everyone else around them think they lead?

4. What are the trappings of leadership where you work? Detail them all – different office space/uniforms/perks etc. Explain how these trappings make you feel about the people you work with and whether they add or detract from any feelings of trust you may have towards them.

5. Are leaders in your organization communicative and approachable? If not, detail how that makes you feel and what effect it has on you when things do not go according to plan.

6. Despite Pugna leading the troupe, their small number makes it possible to have a flat command structure. Pugna is dressed as they are and carries the same equipment. Do you have anything approaching that in your organization? If you did what do you think the challenges would be in making it work? Detail everything you can think of including the disruption caused by the need for additional training.

7. In Chapter I, despite their precautions Pugna's troupe was caught by

surprise at the clearing. They were in new territory, dealing with a lot of new issues. First, detail how your organization deals with new situations on unfamiliar ground. Second, how do you assess Pugna's decision in that moment? What processes does your organization have in place for assessing and then dealing with the unexpected?

8. Do you think Pugna exercised his authority well in that first chapter? Is there anything you would suggest he might have done differently that would have made a difference? Give reasons for your answer.

9. If you were to look at the system of governance of Pugna's tribe how would you describe it? (i.e. Authoritarian, Democratic, etc) How do you think that affected the way events unfolded in this part of the story? State clear reasons establishing cause and effect.

10. Beyond everything covered here, what did you learn in the first Chapter of Pugna's story?

Perception

In Chapter II much of what happens in the story depends upon the perception of Pugna and his men of the people at the other side of the clearing.

1. In your own words explain how you think perception works. How does it affect the way a brand is received by its public? How do you think the awareness of that perception then affects the way a brand behaves?

2. In most cases perception precedes action that arises from an awareness of that perception. This appears to be a chicken and egg question, however actions that arise out of perception suggest that perception is created first, by something other than the immediate action. What do you think that is? List all the things you believe create a perception (gossip, past experiences, reputation etc…) Now look at Chapter II carefully and tick all the elements that you think are present in the perception that leads to the actions of Pugna and his troupe.

3. Do you think that Pugna and his troupe acted correctly in the way they did in the clearing in Chapter II? Would have done something differently had you been in their shoes? What and why?

4. Armed with your knowledge of the impact perception has on conduct and on building trust in general list all the ways you could do things

differently in your business in order to challenge perception and have different outcomes.

5. Looking at your business critically both in terms of its reputation and in terms of all the different parts of it (website, advertising, the ways you communicate, etc) explain in detail how each of these feeds into perception. Assess each element individually and check to see if they all align or if some give a different perception to what you expect, for instance is your website copy friendly and informal yet your terms of use or your FAQs are full of legalese and come across as very formal and maybe, even, forbidding?

6. Detail how your perception of your potential audience affects your communication decisions and even your business decisions.

7. If you need to change the perception that is created about your business detail all the steps you would need to take to achieve that.

8. Does everyone in your organization understand how perception is formed the same way?

9. Does everyone in your organization contribute equally to creating the expected perception of your business?

10. Does anything need to change in your current mode of communication, both internally and externally in order to help you better align the values you hold with your marketing messages?

Assessment

In Chapter III everything that happens hinges on the quality and accuracy of Pugna's assessment of the situation and his evaluation of the Fortis tribe.

1. Identify three moments when Pugna and his men showed human frailty or sensibilities. Explain how, had these moments been handled differently, they would have resulted in different outcomes. Explain what these outcomes might have been and give full justification for your explanation.

2. Detail the process you have in place in your organization that helps you assess external situations, as they occur so that you can formulate the appropriate response.

3. Do you think that the speed at which a situation is assessed plays a pivotal role to how it evolves? Had Pugna and his troupe reacted faster

and tried to resolve everything in half the time would anything have happened differently?

4. A lot of the assessment in any situation takes place in the absence of real data. Explain what happens when you assess a situation without really knowing anything about it. Be detailed with your explanation and back it up with examples.

5. Do you agree with Pugna's approach in analyzing the situation he found himself, and his men, in? How would you have done things differently. Why?

6. What criteria do you think are being used by those who are your intended audience to establish whether your business is trustworthy or not?

7. Do you have a detailed analysis of the assessment a first time customer would do of your business? If not, create a ten-point check of the things they will see if they first come across your online or offline business. Grade each from 1-10 with 10 being the top mark which would convince completely and 1 being the lowest which simply would not. Now, also create ten steps which you would ideally want your first-time customer to see which would convince them that yours is the business they want to be associated with.

8. In Chapter III the assessment of the situation and the Fortis tribe carried out by Pugna was different from that of his men. Explain why you think that was.

9. Explain the effect the mutual throwing of the spears had on you. What did you think would happen at that point of the story? Why? Explain why you think Pugna, reacting instinctively retaliated so quickly and so proportionally?

10. If you had been the leader of the troupe in Pugna's place what would you have done? Why?

Connection

In the final chapter of the story things seem to happen very quickly.

1. Detail all the points of contact that happened between Pugna's troupe and the Fortis tribe. Ascribe a specific value from 1 to 10 to each one with 1 being the lowest point in terms of importance to the story and

10 the highest. Give full explanations why you thought that point was important.

2. Detail all the safeguards that exist in your organization that prevent rush decisions from being taken.

3. Explain how you go about getting real data about any situation in which you need to make a decision.

4. Was there a flaw with Pugna's decision to collect more information about the Fortis tribe? Explain where you think the flaws were and how you would have done things differently in his shoes, and why.

5. Has there been any trust established with the Fortis tribe up to this point? Explain your answer, justify your point of view using quotes from the story and detail the dynamic behind them.

6. What in your opinion changed Pugna's attitude towards the Fortis tribe? What was it that he saw before his men?

7. Detail how your organization gets its humanity across and delivers the message that there are real people behind it?

8. Explain in detail what it is that you do to show that you really care about your business. Then explain in detail what you do to show you really care about your customers. How is this communicated to your target audience?

9. Do you agree with Pugna's assessment of the situation in the final chapter of the story? If you disagree explain your reasons why and then explain what alternative plan of action you would then put in place.

10. Having read the story of the tribe that discovered trust what do you think you have learnt that you did not already know? What would you now do differently in your own communication and marketing?

The Trust Dynamic

In your own words how would you describe the journey of trust that Pugna and his men undertook in their contact and conduct with the Fortis tribe?

If you were to separate it into three distinct stages what names would you give it and what characteristics would each stage have?

Be detailed with your answers. Provide evidence and excerpts from the story to back up what you say. Be prepared, if necessary, to supply extra examples from your own experience.

How would you describe the trust that exists amongst Pugna and his men? Again, give evidence for your answer and supply examples, both from the story and from your own experience, if necessary, to help back it up.

Book II

Trust Works
(the mechanism of Trust)

"*We need people in our lives with whom we can be as open as possible. To have real conversations with people may seem like such a simple, obvious suggestion, but it involves courage and risk.*"
Thomas Moore

1

What is Trust?

Trust is an ethereal quality. Like oxygen or light we notice it only by its absence. Like both oxygen and light it enables us to function in a meaningful, productive way and we generally tend to take it for granted when it's there. The only way to truly understand something we can neither see nor touch is to formalize its definition and look at some of its most noticeable effects. It is through those effects and what they make possible that we can then begin to understand what trust really is and why we need it so badly.

The Oxford English dictionary has no fewer than seven distinct, broad categories which help define what trust is. On the web the page defining it runs to 520 words, not including countless situational examples that demonstrate the meaning of trust in usage. Its lexicographers attempt to nail down one of the most elusive of human qualities, explaining it through usage in the hope that they will somehow define its meaning.

Throughout the ages philosophers, generals, national leaders and literary figures have tried to capture the essence of what trust is. The legendary Lao Tzu believed that trust was a reciprocal arrangement, Nietzsche made it evidence-based, J. M. Barrie, creator of *Peter Pan* thought it was something magical that was either present or it wasn't, Emerson thought it was conceptual rather than circumstantial and Einstein believed the exact opposite. It is J. K. Rowling, however, who in *Harry Potter and the Chamber of Secrets* has one of her characters say: "Never trust anything that can think for itself if you can't see where it keeps its brain" that nails it.

In truth, trust is an emergent quality that comes out of the development of cognitive and psychosocial processes that allow us to establish a sense of the world and our place in it. There are several complex elements to it that require an assessment of potential and actual risk to take place, a quantification of value in the proposed exchange (what is to be directly gained from it) and a calculation of intent. And yes, before I forget, empathy plays a role in there too. Before we can truly trust someone we have to understand them and get a sense of their situation. We need to feel that they too are thinking entities like us, and we need to see both the context of their thinking and how they actually arrive at it. Plus we need to feel that in their actions they also share a degree of vulnerability, just like us. We need, in short, to establish nothing less than a human connection we can feel confidence in.

The real problem with trust and the reason Rowling's description nails it so beautifully is that there is no one type of trust nor one calculation that could tell us how much of it there is and whether the potential exists for more to be created. If that sentence sounds a little loose in its framing consider how trust must have appeared to Kansas University researcher Kim Giffin who in an authored paper in 1967 said: that trust "has been viewed as a somewhat mystical and intangible factor, probably defying careful definition".

In the intervening years we have got no closer to completely nailing down trust but our awareness of the conditions required for its emergence has grown thanks to an accumulating body of data and better digital analysis tools at our disposal.

Why Trust? Why Now?

"The best way to find out if you can trust somebody is to trust them." This is an example of reciprocal trust with an element of faith and perhaps even a hint of wishful thinking in it (or desperation if you have no other choice). It's no surprise that it was said by Ernest Hemingway.

Academic researchers who have spent thousands of manhours looking at how trust is formed in organizational settings are far less sure of its definition as their summation of lengthy papers shows:

" . . . *trust is a term with many meanings.*" – Oliver Williamson
"*Trust is itself a term for a clustering of meanings.*" – Harrison White
" . . . *researchers . . . purposes may be better served . . . if they focus on specific components of trust rather than the generalized case.*" – Robert Kaplan

If they are confused consider the depths of uncertainty the rest of us must swim in, which helps explain the plaintive note struck by an anonymous user on Yahoo Answers who asks: "Why is so difficult to trust someone?" hoping that somehow the wisdom of crowds will combine with the knowledge that resides on the web and provide an answer that can work in almost any situation.

"Because it is" comes back one of the less sympathetic replies.

Family & Relationships > Other - Family & Relationships   Next >

Why is it so difficult to trust someone?

When I think hard about this, I find that it's extremely difficult for me to trust anybody in my life. There isn't one person in my life that I can trust.

I asked a friend of mine today if she could trust anyone and she said to me, "I can trust my boyfriend because he buys me anything I want." I thought that was the most ridiculous thing I've ever heard.

But if you think hard about this, is there anybody you can honestly trust? And why is it so difficult to trust someone?

☆ Follow   ⚐ 6 answers

1.1 Trust is so key to our lives that we turn to anyone, even strangers across the web hoping to find an answer we can understand.

Trust is clearly hard to define. But that is no real answer to the Yahoo user's question. We find trust difficult because we don't always understand

67

what it is that makes it happen. We don't know what makes trust happen because we don't always understand what it is. This is a chain of thought which, when reversed, leads us to conclude that the moment we have a hard definition of trust we can then implement a number of steps to make it manifest. Maybe, but there is a kneejerk and entirely understandable resistance to this thought.

The resistance stems from the fact that trust is at the core of every relational exchange between people. We give our attention to those we have a reasonable expectation to not abuse it. We listen to those we have some expectation will make sense and say something we might benefit from. We interact with those we think are unlikely to hurt us. Without trust nothing would happen. Maybe, we might not even have come out of the caves preferring the misery and restrictions of what we knew to the myriad unknown dangers of the world waiting outside had we not had a sense of trust in our ability to survive through contact with others.

If trust is so truly fundamental to the human condition, we then ask, and we can deconstruct it, are we then not creating a formula for its automatic construction? And if we are doing that is this not going to rob any human interaction from any kind of authenticity and every kind of spontaneity?

That is a very good question to ask, but before we get to it, it is worth examining why trust has become so very critical to us at this point in time.

In the not too distant past that passes for our pre-digital age trust came inherently attached as an unexamined notion, with every relationship we found ourselves in. In that past we had precious little choice. We found ourselves bound in specific groups and specific communities. Our circle of contacts came from work. Locked in silos from which there was no escape we took trust at face value, did not question it because we could not really change it. Even personal relationships, in that world, happened within reach of the gaze of community, family and friends and were therefore hardly dependent upon our judgment of trust, only.

So, in a way trust was associated with physical perception, aided by non-verbal cues, bound my social guidelines or community mores. We knew whether to trust our boss or not, believe in the minister of our local community, accept the tale that one of our siblings told us, believe the story our friends shared down the pub because we were there. We could see the body language, listen to the tonal pitch of their voices, observe the expressions and pick up on nuanced changes which would tell us if the people we already knew were lying to us or not.

The digital world and social media have changed all of this. Through the screens of our phones we can find ourselves in contact with people half a world away, active in communities made up by individuals who themselves come from cultures and backgrounds totally different to ours. In this context we actually have a choice. First of all we choose to be there. Our remotely present, digital selves are the result of conscious decisions and conscious choices made with an awareness of at least some form of intent on our part. Second, all the cues and clues we habitually rely on in order to make our subliminal assessment of trust are absent. Communication takes place in poorly constructed sentences and half-formed thoughts, on the fly, in a hurry, asynchronously with cultural references from dozens of countries thrown in the mix and our attention spread over many different tasks.

This robs us of the ability to instantly judge people based upon perceptions. Assessing their truthfulness uses criteria that we have developed over time, many of which come from direct previous experience from our own social group, but we apply them to situations that no longer have the kind of reality our tools were designed to measure.

In the digital domain trust is now important not only because we really need to know how to trust people and whom to trust but because we need others to trust us and have to learn how to help them do so. No meaningful social media connection is possible and no digital commercial transaction is feasible without trust being present in the mix. And though there is a strong, logical temptation to think that if we somehow 'crack' the trust equation we can then blindly apply it and be done the truth is far from it being so.

Trust has different flavors and types. It changes in every context and each situation even if the participants are the same. As we move forward (as we have already seen in the first part of this book) it is a fluid quality that can be quantified only by its effects. It is as much a part of authenticity as being human and though both authenticity and being human can be faked these days, they cannot really be convincingly faked for very long.

Actions stem from intent. Intent is fashioned from awareness and ethics (which mark the choices we make). Awareness and ethics stem from knowledge and understanding of both content and context. All of this, together, form the stamp that says "Human" and though they can be emulated piece-meal by very clever algorithms, they cannot yet be sustained for any length of time.

The key is consistency. It is consistency that in the past, in the pre-digital world would let us know when someone we knew (and understood) was being less than honest, had a hidden agenda or was trying to hide something by telling partial truths. Consistency is hard to achieve because the variables that must be juggled each time are way too many to accurately calculate or even handle, and they themselves are fluid. Mistakes will be made.

So, knowing how trust is formed and how it can be maintained is not quite the same with knowing how to trick people into trusting you when you're not really worthy of that trust.

The Definition of Trust

As we go through this book we will look at quite a few definitions of trust which will depend upon the situation, its participants, their relationships, their corresponding intent, their reputations and the subject matter. We shall see trust examined as an internal and external force, as a social construct and as an article of faith. There will be degrees of trust being measured in situations where trust appears to have been established but which are still differentiated from other, 'trusted' situations by variables that depend upon expectations, experience and the perception of symmetry in the power coefficient that exists in the relationships between all the different participants.

Depending on how you measure it trust can be psychological, attitudinal, transactional or social. It can be quantified as organizational trust that is very specifically circumscribed or situational trust that knows no boundaries. Its very fluidity is what makes it so versatile and ubiquitous in almost every scenario involving people and relationships.

Ultimately however each and every definition of trust can be boiled down to one specific thing: Confidence. Trust is key to our survival and as such it is an emergent phenomenon that springs from some very basic instincts. Those instincts are there to determine one thing for us and one thing only: is a situation we are about to enter, safe? Do we have confidence that once we launch ourselves in it we will come out the other end relatively intact and capable of going on?

The way we define, establish, calculate and maintain trust then is nothing more than a complex, roundabout, risk-assessment exercise we undertake in order to know what we are letting ourselves in for. If you remember this about trust then you will also realize than no matter how complicated a situation may be, ultimately, the emergence of trust within it springs from the same thing every time: the answer to the question, for the participants in the situation of "is it safe?"

Summary

Trust is noted by its effects and its absence rather than its presence. Researchers agree that it is a necessary part of the human condition. We all intuitively understand the need for trust and have some, unarticulated, idea of its value. None of us want to consciously choose to live in a state of low trust for any length of time. Trust seems then to be almost instinctive in the sense that just like we are hardwired to move away from pain and move towards anything that makes us feel good, low-trust environments make us feel uncomfortable and high trust ones make us feel good.

Five Key Questions To Answer

1. How do you create a sense of trust (and safety) within your organization?
2. How do you then create a sense of trust (and safety) for your customers?
3. How do you reply to questions where a lack of trust is evidently an issue?
4. From a scale of 1 to 10 (with 10 being the highest) rate the trust you have in your employees.
5. From a scale of 1 to 10 (with 10 being the highest) rate the trust you think your organization projects to your customers.

2

The Value of Trust

Trust is valuable because it is perishable and it is unpredictable. It takes a lot of effort to develop and it can be lost in an instant. It can arise out of the confluence of the most unlooked for events and circumstances. In trying to quantify the value of trust we inevitably also see "the story of trust" how it arises in the first instance and how, in our evolutionary journey as humans, has enabled to do things differently, benefiting in the process. In this chapter we shall see some of the ways in which trust is generated and deconstruct some of its key characteristics.

Trust is born with birth. It's made real because of death. Let me explain this a little. Within family groups trust is implicit. While it's never articulated or even discussed in any big way, it is always there. Why? If our sense of trust is born from an inherent articulation of risk assessment to our person, we are at our most vulnerable and helpless at birth, even when we are incapable of really consciously articulating the thought and quantifying the magnitude of our dependence on others. Because we are born inherently weak and helpless and persist in that state for a really long time (from an animal survival point of view) and because we will revert to that stage, as we age, family ties come with an implicit sense of trust that never needs to be articulated and which it is difficult to break.

From this proposition alone we begin to understand that there are three fundamental elements to trust:

- Risk – the sense of danger we are in.
- Identity – the perception of who we are.
- Assurance – the degree to which we are certain of a specific outcome in a given situation.

It is my supposition, and I will back it up with research, throughout the chapter, that these three fundamental elements are at work every time there is a decision we make that involves a transitional state where we go from a position of relative strength to one of inherent weakness.

All three fundamental elements of trust are dependent upon context and they are all filtered through personal, prior experience. The newborn baby, for instance, has few instincts beyond knowing what (or who) is likely to keep it safe and who (or what) will cause it harm. The reaction stimulus that educates it is one of pain and its avoidance and comfort and its desirability. Its prior experience is acquired from the very moment it is born (provided it survives the birth) and accumulates throughout its life as an adult, until its passing.

The baby's parents (primarily) and the extended family group around it act to usually minimize any risk and pain it may feel and maximize any comfort and joy it can enjoy. Growing up in that environment the baby develops into a young adult and, at some point into an adult. At the point of its earliest admission into the family group however the baby is a question mark. A mass of potentialities ring-fenced by unknown unknowns, variables that can't always be foreseen and the effects of which cannot be predicted. There is as much a lack of trust in the baby from the family group's perspective as there would be the other way (if babies knew how to feel trust). But from the family group's perspective the baby does not yet pose a risk, just a potential waste of resources. Without an immediate sense of threat, there is a willingness to at least take a chance and bring the baby up into adulthood.

As it develops the baby assumes the identity that is conferred to it by the family group and that identity makes it a member of a tightly-knit social group whose members are bonded via blood ties and where trust already exists. At the point where the baby grows into a thinking adult (J. K. Rowling's definition of trusting in a thinking entity whose brain is kept somewhere we can see) the trust it has for its family group and the trust given back in return has moved from the risk-assessment area of unknown unknowns to one of solid assurance.

It is of such tiny and inevitable beginnings such as birth, that momentous forces are fashioned. Acorns grow into mighty oaks. The rearing and survival of a newborn develops into a person who is integrated into a group where everything happens because of the presence of something fundamental and invisible. A quality intimately linked to its survival, which is capable of making everything else possible.

There is a direct, connecting line that extends from our home environment and the place where we grew up to the world outside. Our personal experiences, those we can consciously recall and those which formed our subconscious self, now become the primary matrix of expectation we apply to the world when we look at it as a whole and try to determine the answer to the seemingly simple question: who can we possibly trust?

You are right in thinking that everyone's home environment and childhood experiences are different. That's true. They are.

They form a unique mix of memories we carry in our conscious and subconscious minds, as we go through life. Because of them some of us will be more trusting (and perhaps even gullible) and some less so. Some will be better able to calculate risk and determine trust than others. All of us however will measure the world against a benchmark that has its foundation in our earliest life, rooted in our oldest memories, created as we grew up. A benchmark that contains the fundamental criteria of: calculation of Risk, definition of Identity and establishment of Assurance, which we need in order to form trust in a given situation.

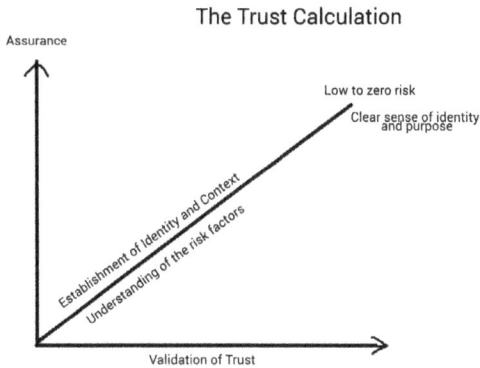

The Trust Calculation

Assurance

Low to zero risk

Clear sense of identity and purpose

Establishment of Identity and Context

Understanding of the risk factors

Validation of Trust

Fig 2.1- *Assurance in a given person or situation grows in direct proportion to the growth of identity of its participants, the clarity of understanding of their roles and the reduction of uncertainty and risk, over time.*

If trust is so fundamental in human relationships that its value is equated to survival and it emerges out of family interactions and bonding from the moment we are born, it might be argued that there is only that moment in life during which we can develop the necessary responses that allow us to learn to trust. But that isn't the case. In our social constructs there are tightly-knit groups where a sense of inherent vulnerability and the realization that we cannot survive on our own also lead to incredibly strong bonds and the development of an unshakable sense of trust amongst individuals.

Writing in *The Well-Being of Nations* a book published by the Organization for Economic Co-Operation and Development (OECD) under the warning that "closely-knit groups may exclude outsiders" subject experts who include the Vice-President of the World bank, Oxford University Dons and the adviser to the Irish prime Minister, write: *"A restricted radius of trust within a tightly knit group, such as family members or closed circles of friends, can promote forms of social interaction that are inward-seeking and less orientated to trust and co-operation at the wider community level (Knack, 1999; Portes and Landholt, 1996). An exclusive focus on group interests to the neglect of wider public interests can promote socially destructive "rent-seeking" activities (Olson, 1982 and Knack, 1999). In companies, strong ties of trust and mutual obligation may, in some circumstances block information from outside and impede innovation (Kern, 1998 and Uzzi, 1997)."*

Concerns about the inward looking aspect of closely-knit groups aside, we can see that besides companies, closed circles of friends and family groups, to the growing list of circumstances or situations where a strong sense of trust can flourish we can now add military institutions or organizations whose members bond into special groups that help them pull through dangerous missions and the inherent risks of the battlefield and even embattled start-ups where the founding members act like a finely-tuned, cohesive, machine. The list is indicative and far from exhaustive and its point is that a strong sense of trust can be generated at moments other than those which gave us birth, particularly when they too are linked to the formation of identity.

The value of trust then, in the first instance is two-fold. First, it gives us as individuals the ability to survive when otherwise we mightn't. In the initial stage of the family group survival is quite literal, as it is in the battlefield, but in most other situations it is metaphorical. This does not make the bond any less real or the quality of trust that is developed any different.

Second, it allows the group we are in to 'absorb' us, giving us an identity that makes us part of it. One of the roles personal identity plays is to define an individual's value to a group so by acting in this fashion the group is looking out for itself as much as for the individual. Viewed as a basic loss/gain differential we can assume that trust significantly lowers the energy expenditure required to get an individual to the point that they can contribute to a group and renders them 'safe' whilst inside it. This in turn maximizes group gains and makes the practice worthwhile.

To illustrate the point consider that if this wasn't the case parents wouldn't have to rear the children they have, their parenting duties would be deemed to be complete as long as they gave them food to keep them alive and shelter to keep them safe from the elements (some of the ape groups do exactly that). Companies wouldn't have to spend large amounts of time and effort in orientation for new employees and in creating a company culture that everyone needs to be part of. Their duties to themselves, as employer would be fulfilled the moment they pointed a new hire to a work station, and explained what the job required. Companies that actually act that way never last long enough to have a tradition or a history.

Trust Me To Cook and Sleep

The link between energy invested and returns on that investment (ROI) transforms the entire concept of trust and why it is necessary into a basic, evolutionary, survival mechanism that's governed by the need to optimize the use of available resources. We've evolved brains that require up to 20% of the body's energy needs to maintain. A considerable part of the brain's cognitive processes is given over to determining the trust that is present in specific situations so there has to be some evidence at least of how we got to "here" from a "there" that is lost in the evolutionary branches of our hominin past.

Admittedly it's a little bit difficult to convincingly go into the past. The fossil record is patchy. We can't even agree when man first discovered the use of fire (one million years ago is the best estimate we have evidence for) so to go deep into our evolutionary history looking for trust might seem like a wild goose chase with no chance of success.

The genetic difference between the human genome and that of the chimpanzee genome indicates a difference of about 1.2%. The bonobo (Pan paniscus), which is the close cousin of chimpanzees (Pan troglodytes), differs from humans to the same degree. The DNA difference with gorillas, another of the African apes, is about 1.6%. Most importantly, chimpanzees, bonobos, and humans all show this same amount of difference from gorillas. A difference of 3.1%. Orangutans (whose genome has now been fully mapped) are 97% identical to humans with a 3% difference that puts them in the same class as baboons.

Given the genetic similarities there are some marked differences between the ape groups as well as between them and humans that have nothing to do with genetic markers and a whole lot to do with social constructs. Anthropologist David Samson of Duke University in Durham, North Carolina, has spent many a sleepless night watching apes, sleep.

Watching an orangutan sleep, on its specially constructed sleeping platform, is like watching a person sleep. Orangutans spend a lot of time in deep sleep, their muscles relaxed, eyelids moving back and forth in REM mode. They change positions frequently, sleeping on their backs or sides.

Baboons, on the other hand, sleep upright, propped against a tree, resting on especially hardened skin on their haunches. Their sleep cycles are interrupted by the slightest noise, their minds constantly alert for danger. Baboons and orangutans are of interest here because they both belong to the large-body apes group. Yet they display diametrically opposite behavior when it comes to how they deal with the part of the day when sleep comes and they are vulnerable.

Orangutans, solitary by nature, form loose, widely spaced communities where learning behavior is important. Their non-territorial attitudes allow them to exist in spaces where the competitive drive is reduced to very specific aspects (like fighting for females, between males). Young orangutans are highly social, establishing bonds with same gender and age mates and it is only as they mature that the males become solitary.

Baboons on the other hand live hyper-competitive, aggressive lives and form large groups, known as troops, with as many as 200 individuals in each one, many of whom will spend their entire lives living within 100 feet of each other. Baboons tend to sleep closely together, their fretful sleep interrupted, we fancy, by constant fears and dark imaginings. Each noise signaling, perhaps, a potential predator sneaking up on them, in the dark.

The sleeping habits of apes are of direct concern to us because the quality of sleep primates (including man) enjoy, has recently been acknowledged to give an evolutionary competitive advantage. Armchair science tells us this is common sense. Keep your rival awake the day before a critical presentation and the chances are you will nail it way more convincingly than him. In the wild, consistently good quality sleep is even more important than in the boardroom. Not only does the body get to relax, repair and grow but the brain gets to switch off its conscious part of it so that the subconscious side kicks in to do vital housekeeping tasks that aid learning and make us smarter.

Dr Samson and colleague Robert Shumaker of Indiana University in Bloomington, in the US, did more than armchair science, going out in the field to study the behavior of large bodied apes. Orangutans, who fashion a sleeping platform to support their weight and secure them away from predators on the treetops, enjoyed a better quality of sleep than the highly-strung baboons, who never mastered the skill.

Better quality of sleep positively affects cognitive ability and as Dr Samson noted "From an evolutionary perspective, just as the transition from tree branches to sleeping platforms had adaptive benefits, so too did the early hominin transition from sleeping platforms to secure ground sleep." What is important here of course are the conditions or the qualifying factors this possible in the first place.

The hyper-competitive baboon culture makes it difficult to create an environment with a perception of safety and trust. Baboons constantly square off against each other in a never-ending battle for rank that guarantees better status within the group and greater access to food and females. As a result, despite their seemingly highly organized troop structure, each individual has to rely exclusively on his own resources and hope that when they are asleep and at their most vulnerable, there will be safety in numbers. Worse than that, their brains, stunted by lack of quality sleep are in a state of constant alert, suffering from stress not dissimilar to that felt by humans engaged in high-pressure tasks. The difference is that for a baboon, that is his entire life. Unable to switch off at night, trapped in what he perceives to be a world of constant threat, sleep, the point at which he should be at his most peaceful, is when he is most vulnerable and when he also feels under the most stress.

The seemingly solitary orangutans, on the other hand, trust in the overall safety of their arboreal community, high in the trees, where a widely spaced community beds down for the night. They allow sleep to relax them both physically and mentally, much as we do.

In a not too dissimilar primate setting, Felix Warneken, Associate Professor of Social Sciences at Harvard University, has been busy carrying out an entirely different experiment where he's testing chimpanzee's preference for cooked over raw food and their understanding of the difference between the two. An expansion of the experiment teaches chimpanzees to cook potatoes. Cooked food is acknowledged to be a better resource, it is easier to digest and it's more energy and nutrient-rich so it too offers an evolutionary advantage. Nine, separate, experimental studies published in one paper in the Proceedings of the Royal Society B agree "That there is preliminary evidence that chimps may understand the transformation process, that something currently raw is later cooked."

Cooking is a highly complex cognitive activity that hinges on social structure. In order to do it not only do you need to understand the transformative process involved in the act of cooking itself but you also need to be analytical enough to put several ingredients together. It requires that you defer the instant gratification of eating raw food the moment you get it, so that you can cook it later. It involves complex planning and an awareness of the future not just in terms of meals but also, on a grander scale, in relation to seasons, farming and agricultural food production.

Chimps have the brainpower to understand the nature of cooking and can learn to cook when shown but not the social structure that would make this a sensible thing to do (assuming they could use fire). The positive reinforcement from a taste and nutrition point of view is the same for them as it is for humans. Here's the rub: In the wild Chimps are extremely competitive when it comes to food. There is strong motivation to consume food you have found there and then otherwise a dominant member may just come along and steal it.

In other words, our closest relatives have the brain power needed to cook food, but left to themselves they would never use it. For them, it's better to be a bit more selfish and impulsive when it comes to food.
"Even if you have the cognitive skills to cook food, if the mutual trust isn't there, these skills cannot be used in a meaningful way to become a critical component of human life," says Warneken.

The creation of sleeping platforms and the discovery of cooking food, represent two separate instances in man's evolutionary journey in which the deciding factor was trust. They are points which added their weight to the branching off in the evolutionary tree, allowing us to make evolutionary leaps that got us to the point where we can read books about it all, while the baboon and the chimp are still inching along, their cognitive skills barely shifting, their days spent in search of the food they need that provides them with the energy to survive, the brains stunted from an overload of stress lack of quality sleep.

It may seem circumstantial. We lack the direct evidence perhaps that says trust is exactly what made the difference and looking at the past runs the risk that we interpret everything from the perspective of the present. True as that may be it doesn't change the underlying reality of what we are. Biologically we are open systems. Everything we do and everything we can become, from a physical point of view, depends upon our ability to strike a balance in our energy needs. We cannot, for instance, develop into anything that would physically require an overabundance of energy to run, if we have no means of getting that energy in the first place.

Our 3lb brain consumes almost 20% of the energy available to our body so there has to be a way to gain energy without spending all day foraging and if we have an organ that is so energy intensive there must be a means for it to optimize its performance and give us back a good return on our investment. Cooked food and a good night's sleep fulfill both these requirements.

Social trust enabled man to not only fashion sleeping platforms to comfortably and safely support his larger frame in the trees (which must have meant that suddenly being physically bigger was not a problem).

Initial or mutual trust (the type of trust that makes us, irrationally, trust strangers) then enabled the complex planning that allowed man to transition from a tribe of hunter-gatherers whose fate depended on external factors to an agricultural society where complex, planned outcomes could be put into motion.

When trust has played such a pivotal role in our evolutionary history it is the closest thing to an instinct we have. Learnt from birth, the question is how does our contextual knowledge of it that's shaped by our social upbringing within a tightly-knit group allows us to extend it its definition to satisfactorily cover situations that are unlikely to ever come even close to the sense of trust we've experienced in those tightly-knit groups?

Just going for a walk down the street, for instance, has enough known unknowns and unknown unknowns to suddenly become an enterprise fraught with terrible ambiguities. Will the strangers I pass by attack me? Will they think I could attack them and pre-empt me? How do I signal the fact that I mean them no harm without suddenly becoming vulnerable to attack myself because of it? Hanging on these questions are answers that can be applied equally well to business and eCommerce as well as politics and life, which is why a lot of research time (and money) has been spent on them.

Trust, Rationality and Social Duty

David Dunning, a psychology professor at Cornell University and his colleagues, say that all rational behavior theories predict that people shouldn't trust complete strangers. In situations where we are faced with a complete unknown we have nothing to help us predict which way things will go. Any rational model of behavior predicts that no matter what the other person promises, he will renege the instant it is in his interest to do so.

The moment our back is turned, we fear, we may not be allowed to continue our walk in peace. Now that they have our money, the package we expect from the online retailer, will never arrive. The person that's promised to back us in a tight spot won't do so the moment the going gets tough. As a matter of fact everything we have learnt about the sources of trust so far indicates that in the absence of knowledge about another person we are incapable of carrying out any reasonable assessment of risk and we therefore should rationally assume that we simply can't trust them.

Yet there is a paradox associated with trust that makes it all the more interesting. Despite the fact that logic tells us that we should not trust anyone, in any situation where the unknown variables are too many or the risks too high, we nevertheless go ahead and take what can only be called a leap of faith. The researchers described this as "a psychological state comprising the intention to accept vulnerability based on the chance of reward from positive intentions or behavior of another."

The felicity of this response led to the birth of eBay on the 4th September 1995, when Pierre Omidyar, the man who found the company, sold a broken laser pointer for $14.83 and made it the first eBay transaction on record.

Dunning was aware of the irrational tendency in us when it came to trust but not its prevalence or rationale. He decided to delve deeper. In a series of trust experiments with 645 undergraduates, the scientists found that 62% would give away a small sum of money even if their two options were that the other person would keep it all, or, if the person decided to return it, both would get back a larger amount. This excessive amount of trust is not connected in any way with the way we first experience trust as individuals. Its apparent irrationality has roots elsewhere and cannot be attributed to family life, closely-knit group dynamics or a weird upbringing.

There is a dimension to trust that has nothing to do with our expectation of social norms. Excess trust, hypothesized the researchers, is due to a widely felt socially acceptable mandate that we show respect for the other person's character, presuming the other person has sufficient integrity and goodwill even if we do not believe it privately. If this sounds facile it's because it is. It's a response that feeds into perception but perception has a way of guiding what we do as a result and, in this fashion, shaping reality.

These are all dots being joined and, thankfully, there are many eyes and minds looking at each one. Christopher Berger, a doctoral student at the Department of Neuroscience at the Karolinska Institutet, in Sweden, was convinced that reality would not be affected if perception changed. He too decided to test his conviction. In a study conducted by his researchers where he presented subjects with specific scenarios and fed them highly detailed accounts of imagined events he found that not only perception could change reality, affecting the way the subjects responded to real situations but imaginings could seriously affect outcomes by altering the perception of the subjects and introducing unreasonable expectations or paranoid fears.

When imagination can change perception and perception can change reality it follows that an internal model of a world where expectations are dismal is likely to lead to real-world outcomes that are equally bad. If we do meet as strangers in the street and I really think there is a good chance you might attack me, everything about me, from my body language to the telltale marks of my preparation to fight you, to my facial expressions, will lead you to conclude that I am a risk to you. Unless one of us turns tail and runs, we will fight. Our way of overcoming this inevitable spiral into dismal outcomes arising from fear-based expectations and dark imaginings, it seems, is to inject a level of excess trust into a scenario that borders on the irrational but which, as it turns out, shapes reality to a more palatable version of what we expect it to be.

If we really feel that we have a social duty to think the best of others and actually feel guilt when we don't (as the researchers discovered) does this mean that we actually balance in our heads two separate types of trust mechanisms at once? One type of trust springing from the rationality of our experience in the safe environment of the family group, the tight bonding that has withstood the assurance test over a large span of time and a very different type of trust springing from a willingness to extend the sense of safety we've known in our family group, out, onto the broader world we encounter beyond it?

Do we set out from home to make the world our family? Is it our wish that it was so? It would appear to be the answer. There are not two, incompatible types of trust in our head. We carry with us the one and same type of trust we start out with from birth and project it in the only rational way we can to safeguard not just our person, but also our sense of sanity.

That's an assertion we can test. If trust is key and it starts at birth through extended, detailed contact with our immediate family group dysfunctional families will give rise to members who are caught in an internal tug of war. On the one hand they want to trust, fervently projecting their innermost desire onto the world outside, perhaps more than people with a more fortunate upbringing. On the other the damage wrought by their experiences will have them locked in guilt, fear and anger. Guilt because they cannot quite bring themselves to trust others (and they feel they should), fear to extend trust towards anyone, and anger because they find themselves, unfairly, caught between these two responses.

Writing on that same subject in *Toxic parents: Overcoming their hurtful legacy and reclaiming your life* a book that's rarely been off the best-seller lists since it was first published in 1989, psychotherapist, Dr Susan Forward, details how a dysfunctional family and poor parenting contribute to the creation of individuals with huge trust issues and a poor concept of personal identity. People who find it difficult to function in the world with the same degree of positive expectation of outcomes as the majority of us.

The good news is that despite the apparent damaged nature of these individuals most will and do find their way back to a more balanced approach. Their experiences along with the help of friends as well as professionals they meet along the way, helping them overcome the issues caused by their upbringing.

If we are to call the type of trust we learn from birth, which we apply to direct personal experiences within a select group of people, personal trust then it becomes the pathway through which we learn to assess, extend and use trust in the wider world, what we might want to call universal trust because of its generic and highly customizable nature. The first becomes the stepping stone for the second with the same certainty that night follows day. There are four distinct elements to the personal type of trust we acquire as we grow up which can be broken down and analyzed. Since they are situational and experiential they stem from direct contact and assessment, weighing and deciding.

Without further ado they are:

- Context – What is it that requires trust?
- Assurance – What will it take to establish, maintain and even extend trust?
- Validation – How frequently is assurance of trust required?
- Trust – Is it present in at least a small, initial measure? Can it now be given?

These four elements then map onto four distinct (and familiar) steps from which universal trust arises in every situation:

- Contact – What's the content and context of the initial approach towards us?
- Perception – What is the mutual expectation here?
- Assessment – How will we test and then weigh the honesty, authenticity and intent of the participants?

- Connection – Having successfully negotiated the previous three steps a base level of trust must now be given.

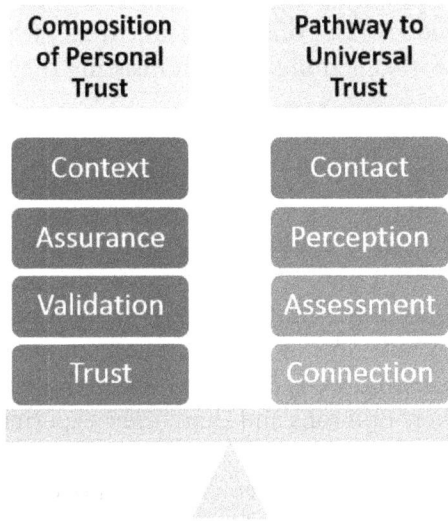

Composition of Personal Trust	Pathway to Universal Trust
Context	Contact
Assurance	Perception
Validation	Assessment
Trust	Connection

Fig 2.2 - *There is a delicate balance in how we experience trust personally, which then allows us to extend it with confidence to the world beyond our immediate senses.*

It may seem odd, when mentioning the composition of trust, to include trust as an element in building itself but as J. F. Barrie himself said trust is either there or it isn't and if it's absent creating it is a truly uphill struggle, so we will have to include it, at least in the sense that it has to exist in an initial phase once the three steps preceding it are satisfactorily concluded.

Modes of Trust

Historically, as we've seen, evolutionary leaps have been made possible because trust was there. That trust, at the beginning, had not yet had time to build up validation or find assurance. The trust given in that initial phase therefore had to be a rudimentary extension of hope, a psychological probing of circumstances that we shall label "initial trust". This initial trust springs from a rationally sound foundation. Leaping out of bed in the morning you can look out the window and expect that no one is going to be outside it, planning to attack your house.

This is the kind of mutual trust that researchers could not find evidence of in chimpanzee societies which results in them living in fear and suspicion. Its lack of it is holding them back from cooking food, even if they know how. This type of trust is based upon the same kind of mutual perception that gives the benefit of the doubt to strangers and allows mutually beneficial transactions like the initial leap of faith that gave birth to eBay, to take place. We could also call this "face value trust" where we simply take someone's word for something without insisting they prove themselves worthy.

This kind of trust springs from the well of personal trust that's developed over time as we grow up. As such it is intensely personal and personalized. The real world however does not function strictly in this fashion. Instead of a linear connection from us to whatever scenario or person we need to extend trust to next there is the interjection of many other variables. We are connected to a constant flow of information from neutral sources, TV, newspapers, the internet and we are part of extended social networks where others openly voice their opinions and share their experiences with us.

Trust cannot, in the real world, be just a matter of personal choice. Intuitively we know that there has to be another mode of at work.

Sure enough, there are at least two. In addition to the "initial or personal trust" that stems directly from us, there is the trust we extend after we receive a recommendation from a trusted individual. Let's call that "associative trust". When a friend recommends a particular type of pen to me as suitable for writing on any surface I am more willing to take the required leap of faith and purchase it on the strength of the recommendation alone.

Such is the nature of trust that both initial trust and associative trust are temporary states. They are the "perception" stage of our four-step trust equation where assessment and then connection (via assurance that trust is warranted) are still ahead of us in the contact timeline.

The moment initial and associative trust are validated by personal experience or by any other validating mechanism we have set up we now have a historical context which leads directly to reputation building. Reputation is based on the trust experience of others when that experience is shared openly. In a slightly more formalized definition, reputation represents the willingness of someone to extend trust to an organization or person they have no direct experience of, reputational trust.

In a social media as well as a business setting reputation is what allows an efficiency of scale to take place and a scaling of connections to occur. In social groups reputation is frequently equated with popularity, in social media with fame and in business settings with trustworthiness. In each of these cases it leads to people becoming more willing to connect with you and give you their trust.

It is clear from this that trust, to emerge, requires an awareness of context and a set of expectations that emerge from that awareness. Trust then is not just situational, arising out of the particular context of a particular scenario but it is also subjective, dependent upon the perception of importance an individual places upon an activity. To explain this a little more simple consider that if you are buying a box of matches, you think nothing of spending a few cents to purchase one from a street vendor you've never seen before. The question of match quality, expiry date and even if every single match in the box will light up (or if the number of matches stated on the box exactly matches what's inside it) do not rank very highly in your filtering mechanism because the cost of a box of matches is minimal and they are easy to come by. The worst thing that can happen is that only a few matches in the box will work. It can be annoying but not catastrophic. Typically you also do not expect a match vendor to be a highly skilled professional doing a difficult job which is why your expectation of the transaction is relatively low.

Yet, you wouldn't think of buying prescription medicines from a street vendor no matter how convincing his qualifications as a chemist, might be or how attractive the price. We attach a high qualitative value to prescription medicines and the risk associated with getting that wrong is high so we automatically raise the bar when it comes to doing due diligence by requiring a more complex number of steps that lead to assurance. We need, for instance, a chemist, someone who is behind the counter who actually looks and sounds like they know what they are doing. There is a procedure associated with getting (and checking) a prescription (which is why we fully expect the chemist to verify the prescription and we put up with the inconvenience as they do so) and a set of externally imposed checks and controls that are designed to help us feel that everything in this context is the result of some validating process.

The pharmacy itself is a solid building with a specific set up cost. It is in a shopping center or part of a set of other shops in a city and serves countless other individuals (not just ourselves). Its existence requires a permit, it did not just spring up yesterday, there is tangible, verifiable historical context applied to it. The individual working behind the dispensing counter is highly trained and has passed a set of qualifying exams. The list can get extremely comprehensive with ever increasing granularity being added to it so you get the picture. You also realize why appearances are important, particularly when it comes to setting up a new business or a new website and how those appearances must take into account not just the expertise of the people who are setting up the business but also the set of expectations held by their potential audience.

The moment we get past personal trust, every other kind of trust is governed by steps that are subject to detailed analysis. For that reason I am not going to touch upon reputational trust which we talked about earlier, just yet. This chapter is still about exploring the fundamentals and better understanding the story of trust itself.

Fig 2.3 - *To understand the importance of context and identity in trust-based relationships consider that if you don't know who you are and have no idea how you got here it becomes impossible to know whom to trust.*

We've come some way. We've seen that trust, just like life is forced upon us unasked. We accept it because we have no choice and it makes things just work. From birth to adulthood we accumulate, refine and constantly use trust. We intuitively understand the value of trust, yet, when something is so fundamental that we barely have a definition for it despite the fact that it has now been intensely studied for nearly half a century the suggestion is that we are perhaps missing something.

We are looking at things too closely or not closely enough. We perhaps lack the current language necessary to describe what we are seeing. Trust, as we shall see is fragmented. It has many different types and flavors, arises from a myriad different contexts and can exist in even the most constrained situations where the trust in question is negative (as in trusting someone to not do something they are supposed to).

Its complexity closely reflects the human condition. Which leads us perhaps to the opening sentence of this chapter. Birth we can understand, but death. We have no choice. At some point the sum total of who we are and what we have become will begin to fail. The organic systems that keep us together will degrade to the point where keeping us alive is not something they can do. Just like birth this is not something we can consciously choose. This too is fostered upon us.

If we are fortunate our passing will be peaceful, uneventful and will happen amongst family. More often than not it takes place in hospices or hospitals, surrounded by medical technology and highly expert strangers. In either case we are, again, helpless and vulnerable. Our sense of dignity and remaining life left in the hands of others. The only difference is that this time round, at least, we have a bedrock of experience which allows us to realize that we have consciously decided to trust our fate in the hands of others. If trust is born unlooked for with our birth, it acquires for us, a final concrete form with our death.

Summary

When something is as fundamental as trust the danger is that everyone thinks they understand what it is and therefore fail to define it. Trust research has suffered from this perception. Those who had a sociological background, for example, would look at trust as a social quality, needed to help social structures be built and then function. Psychologists have looked at it as a cognitive mechanism designed to allow the brain to make rational choices in seemingly irrational situations. Marketers have looked at it as a set of transactional safeguards and lawyers have regarded it as a set of mutually deterrent clauses designed to establish a set of assurances for two distrusting parties to overcome their distrust of each other and work together.

Because trust is invisible, because it is hard to even articulate and even harder to quantify at times, because it morphs depending upon the mindset, expertise and occupational bias of the person who happens to be looking at it, it is hard to put a dollar value on it that makes sense to a balance sheet or a board of directors or a company CEO or an entrepreneur or a single marketer looking at his screen late at night and feeling the pressure of making things happen so he can pay the rent.

Well, how does $28 billion dollars sound? Which is the share value Volkswagen (VW) lost in just four days when the story broke of their lying on the emissions of their cars (about which we shall talk in detail later in the book). Or how does 433 billion euros sound which is the value of the interdependent economy that has grown around VW in Germany and which it may also now be in jeopardy?

Next time someone thinks about the value of trust they should really remember that it's a little like the price of oxygen. It is almost zero, until you haven't got it any more, Then it becomes priceless.

Five Key Questions to Answer

1. Articulate your own personal definition of trust.
2. Detail one instance which you can provide as an example of trust action.
3. Using the four steps that show how universal trust is created, explain how your business or brand utilize them successfully.
4. Is there an instance where your business or brand can improve upon to help engender more trust?
5. Describe the process you would use to carry out a business transaction your company or brand routinely engage in, if there was no trust in the equation.

3

Trust at Zero Acquaintance

Trust always implies a relationship of some sort. We experience trust in the bonds we form with the people we know and the companies we do business with. We have trust in the technology brands we use and food and beverages we buy. Trust underpins every transaction we enter into and every engagement we become part of. Yet trust, somehow, must start from somewhere. There has to be something that makes us trust at the zero moment of first acquaintance when even our complex trust mechanisms have zero data to crunch and cannot therefore calculate anything. The rational approach to trust implies that these zero moments are full of distrust. Yet, this is not the case. In this chapter we shall see exactly why. We shall examine the reason a certain amount of irrational behavior actually is the norm, rather than the exception and we shall learn about three basic types of trust.

There is a song called *Trust Me* by The Fray; a Denver, Colorado rock band whose lyrics contain the lines:

I found a friend or should I say a foe
Said there's a few things you should know...

If I say who I know it just goes to show
You need me less than I need you
But take it from me we don't give sympathy
You can trust me trust nobody

Within them is contained the entire dilemma facing us whenever we happen to stand alone, strangers in a strange place, looking out at the world and trying to decide where to place our trust. Philosophers such as the Italian Niccolò Machiavelli and the English Thomas Hobbes have considered this type of situation carefully. Born some 119 years apart in different countries and very different cultures they nevertheless agreed in their counsel to their readers against trust. Their take was that if recipients of trust are rational actors serving exclusively their own self-interest, they have every reason to exploit trust as soon as it is in their interest to do so. Thus, one should never offer one's trust unless the other person's response is placed under such heavy constraints or sanctions that the person is compelled to honor it.

These were both intelligent, influential men. Their critical thinking served them well in their chosen careers and their writings are still with us, today. Conditioned to look for a reason that explains (and then ensures) personal survival they based everything they wrote on their observations of political and social conditions during a century when Europe experienced tremendous upheaval.

Their rationalist's approach of looking at the world suggests a strict sequence of demonstrable cause-and-effect events that need to take place in any situation for trust to arise. However logical this approach may seem it has a significant flaw: it doesn't take into account the moment of zero acquaintance. The zero acquaintance level offers a slate that is equally blank for two parties to connect in. This is moment of ambivalence The Fray sing of: when you don't know anything about the other party you're about to enter into a transaction with all reciprocal constraints that Machiavelli and Hobbes recommend be put in place are non-existent. All bets are off.

What's more, any suggestion of constraints at that point is more likely to raise the red flags of concern than have the opposite effect. Imagine coming across a commercial website where within seconds of you having landed there you are asked to securely input your credit card details to "register serious intent" or entering a bricks and mortar business where the very first sign that greets you as you enter says in big red letters "No Time Wasters". Bizarre as it may seem I have come across both examples, one being an art website and the other a shop selling souvenirs on Scarborough Beach in Perth, Western Australia. I have no idea what the traffic was on the art website but the souvenir shop was empty and seeing how, when on holiday I do nothing but waste time, I did not remain in it for very long, either.

Yet all of us have spent time browsing on commercial websites which we have no experience of and all of us have entered bricks and mortar stores on a whim, even if they were not part of a branded chain we knew anything about.

Our willingness to actually place trust in a seemingly irrational situation and enter into a transaction with someone we have no knowledge of is what makes trust such a paradoxical phenomenon. While we have seen already that trust is a risk-assessment mechanism that looks to minimize potential risks to ourselves and maximize the potential rewards we can receive when it comes to that initial contact our tendency is to inherently trust rather than distrust.

The reason for that lies in our recognition of the impossibility (and perhaps the undesirability) of transactional paralysis that would arise as a direct result of the effect of distrust in such a situation. The world we live in is one of opportunities and possibilities. It works because we sense that there is a motive force driving things forward of which we are part of. Buying street food in NYC, stopping by a roadside farmer's market to buy some fruit, starting a conversation with a stranger at a party and buying a T-shirt we really liked in an online unique design store are all perfect examples of our willingness to extend trust to strangers.

The reason why we are willing to engage so openly in what is admittedly risky behavior lies in the social context within which this contact takes place. It's not that Machiavelli and Hobbes are dismal human beings or happened to perhaps see humanity only at its worst. Their advice in the social context of their times made perfect sense. That same advice, given to a traveler passing by one of the war-devastated cities of Fallujah, in Afghanistan, also makes perfect sense.

Law and order and social norms have mostly collapsed there. Trusting strangers when you have a choice not to, is not a wise course of action.

Street food vendors in NYC however are part of the same extended, complex and structured social order as farmers' roadside markets and unique T-shirt design online shops. In other words we understand that there is a structured social order we each part of. The norm, in that environment is for trust to be given rather than withheld and not giving it makes one antisocial rather than a fool who's been taken advantage of.

Morton Deutsch, working on the psychology of trust for Bell Labs in the 70s, famously wrote "to be distrustful is morally far more flagrant than to be credulous. To sin is less virtuous than to be sinned against". He was making a point about conditions. At the transactional level where zero information is available trust becomes a predictive mechanism of human behavior based upon an awareness of context.

In other words, none of us really want to appear to be distrusting and be accused of unfairly suggesting someone should not be worthy of our trust just because we don't have direct knowledge of them. The implicit suggestion here is that the societies we live in, in the modern world, depend heavily upon our giving the benefit of the doubt to strangers and bridging the faith gap in first instances as part of a wider social contract.

Should the Zombie Apocalypse happen (or should we indeed, be in Fallujah when all-out war has broken out,) the social norm changes and we indeed should not do business with anyone who cannot offer the type of guarantees we expect to see, upfront.

Barring those conditions however, what seals the deal of our initial trust-based reaction in almost every other type of situation is the fact that we know that without trust flowing 'magically' through our social constructs it is impossible for any government to survive, no political institution can work and no social group can flourish.

This would suggest that within normal social conditions trust is both pervasive and inevitable. Reinhard Bachmann, Professor of International Management, School of Oriental and African Studies (SOAS), University of London, UK and Akbar Zaheer, Curtis L. Carlson Chair in Strategic Management, Carlson School of Management, University of Minnesota, US suggest as much in their *Handbook of Trust Research* where after meticulously compiling research from across the spectrum and editing it all into a 400 page volume, they conclude that: "Trust exists, not only in special interpersonal, social relations, but also in business arrangements and economic transactions."

Paul C. Adams an Associate Professor and Director of Urban Studies at the Department of Geography and the Environment at University of Texas at Austin, applies various geographical lenses to communication as an element of individual experience. In his book *The Boundless Self: Communication In Physical And Virtual Spaces* he writes:

> "*Because self-serving behavior, anomie, hostility, and other manifestations of distrust lie behind many of the dysfunctions of large societies, it is easy to overlook the pervasiveness of trust. But it is the general prevalence of trust that makes the presence of any of these forms of nontrust so devastating.*"

Yet as yet another researcher, Diego Gambetta, an Italian born social scientist and a professor of social theory at the European University Institute in Florence and an official fellow at Nuffield College, University of Oxford, so eloquently says:

> *This very pervasiveness of trust seems to have generated less analysis than paralysis: in the social sciences the importance of trust is often acknowledged but seldom examined, and scholars tend to mention it in passing, to allude to it as a fundamental ingredient or lubricant, an unavoidable dimension of social interaction, only to move on to less intractable matters.*

Making Trust Happen

If trust is truly as unavoidable and pervasive as everyone suggests, if against all rational reason it is our first instinctive reaction in moments of Zero Acquaintance provided we live in a socially normal environment, what exactly are the steps required to make it happen?

To examine that we need to do one more thing: understand that trust is not just based upon a shared understanding of social norms but also a shared understanding of language and a framework of communication. Language and communication cannot work without trust that goes beyond reason and affect.

This is what the American legal scholar Ian Roderick Macneil has argued in what he calls his "essential contract theory" where he defines a relational contract as a contract whose effect is based upon a relationship of trust between the parties involved so that the explicit terms of the contract are just an outline and there are implicit terms and understandings which determine the behavior of the parties.

A ".. contract between totally isolated, utility maximizing individuals is not [a] contract, but war; contract without language is impossible; and contract without social structure and stability is -quite literally- rationally unthinkable, just as man outside society is rationally unthinkable'.

At some level, even the dishonest have to mean what they say.

> *"When Saddam Hussein broke a fundamental ethical convention by using his own citizens as a shield against attack, he still had communicate this to the enemy, and adhere to what is meant by the term 'citizen', for his threat to have the intended effect."*

Without the means to say something in a way that makes us commonly understood there can be no trust (which means, I suppose, that should Aliens from outer space ever come to Earth, they'd better have great Babel Fish or speak a Terran language if they want us to trust them).

So the very first requirement for trust to occur is communication. This is The Fray's aptly expressed: *If I say who I know it just goes to show/You need me less than I need you* is not only a framework being put in place for communication to take place but, wisely perhaps, they're already establishing a social pecking order, namedropping to show that when it comes to relationships this may be an asymmetrical one with power leaning their way. Trust the person in their song or leave them the hell alone.

We don't quite have to go that far. Communication is sufficient in the first instance and it can take many forms. From content on a web page to a sales call to an email message to advertisement on a billboard. Irrespective of format the requirement is that the language used, its complexity, tone, style and method need to become the first step towards establishing that first contact, laying down the groundwork that will bridge any perceived trust gap.

Effective communication creates the framework within which everything else takes place. Trust, in any form is manifested when, within the established framework, these four basic steps take place:

- Contact
- Perception
- Assessment
- Connection

These four steps are present, in the background of every trust-based scenario and if trust is "pervasive and inevitable" then they are too.

If communication creates the framework within which trust happens and the four steps above create the points through which trust is manifested it goes to reason that trust, the invisible quality that flows through every social construct we have, also has to have some core components we can actually measure. This is critical requirement if we are to establish any kind of benchmark for trust to be assessed in different scenarios.

I said that trust is a spontaneously generated quality that begins in familial relationships when vulnerability is at its maximum and choice is non-existent. Outside those relationships there are a lot of socially constructed mechanisms (the law, peer group pressure, workplace norms, social acceptability and reputational values, to mention just a few) which mitigate the risk and create a more symmetrically balanced relationship between two parties.

Every relationship is then governed by motive, capability and reliability and these three factors become the core components of the trust equation:

$$T = \frac{M+C}{R}$$

T trust
C credibility
R reliability
M motive

Fig 3.1- *When we know a person (or institution well) calculating the amount of trust we place in them becomes relatively easy. We know what their capabilities are, understand their motives and know whether they are reliable or not.*

Trust then is calculated through:

- **Motive** – in a person it helps explain their behavior. Why they act the way they do. In an organization or institution it helps define the way they operate. When we are unfamiliar with the person or the institution this is the hardest component of trust that we can divine.
- **Capability** – this reflects the ability to do something specific in the task at hand. An online website that sells books and ships them all over the world, for instance, has to be capable of doing exactly that. A person that offers to help me do my taxes has to have some level of skill in filling out tax forms.
- **Reliability** – the simplest measure of reliability is dependability. A person or business, an organization or institution has to be able to deliver what they promise and do so consistently, time and again. We would never buy from Amazon if the chances of what we bought reaching us were only 50%. Amazon, in particular, has gained incredible global market share by commoditizing the shopping experience, turning the impersonal contact that a person with a computer has on their website into a consistent, almost mundane transaction where the three components being examined here can be taken for granted to the effect that they can become invisible and be forgotten about. Amazon, wants us to feel it's family!

To illustrate the way these components change each time consider that my brother (a family member whom I trust without thinking) may ask me to let him help me get a little more sleep by writing a chapter of this book for me. I understand his motives (he is concerned about my health and wants to help me) and he is reliable so I know he will do it. But he is not a writer and has certainly never done any research of any kind so his capability in this case is under question and my trust in him to complete such a task to the requirements of my editor is, indeed, low.

Similarly an eBay seller (to change scenario) who has a rating of 98.8% when others in the same class go over the 99.5% mark may have what I need in terms of merchandise and price (so their capability is not in question). I understand their motive for selling the merchandise but if the feedback indicates that it is of poor quality or does not arrive as advertised their reliability drops and makes it unlikely that I will be becoming a customer of theirs.

Fig 3.2 - *Although relatively high as an overall percentage the low rating for its class of this eBay seller coupled with the large number of negative reviews over a one-month period makes his reliability questionable.*

Trust then is not just a volatile quality that can vary from one relationship to the next or even in the same relationship as the situation changes. It also comes with contextual variations which allow it to be broken down into specific elements for particular settings.

We will go on and examine them now, but it is worth remembering that the four points through which trust is manifested and the three components at its core are, ultimately what trust is all about, always.

Three Types of Trust

It's not always possible to create a personal, personable relationship The Fray's unknown person in the song namedrops, delivers a sense of not being in need. *Trust me if you want*, he suggests, *or not. I don't care.*

Everybody cares. When trust breaks down the relationship sours. Mistrust leads to suspicion. Suspicion leads to hostility. No one wins. So, depending on the situation there are three ways that a relationship based trust can work:

- Deterrence Based Trust
- Knowledge Based Trust
- Identification Based Trust

99

You can be clever with these and shrink them down to DBT, KBT or IBT but you'd better know what they are each time you use them and what makes them work the way they do. Each of these types of trust is important enough to warrant a separate look.

Deterrence Based Trust (DBT)

In the early days of eBay merchants, keen to build their reputation would quite blatantly say "we will give positive feedback after receiving yours". Merchants and eBay buyers, at the time were keen to build their reputation because it made transactions easier. A stellar rating increased the level of trust between parties and it added a certain degree of pride in the achievement.

While the suggestion that someone you have bought something from and already paid for it would only give you feedback after they have received yours, sits well with the self-serving behavior that Machiavelli and Hobbes would recognize as the norm for their time, it is antithetical to the kind of world we want to build today.

The eBay team thought so too and soon changed the guidelines to explicitly ban any kind of behavior like that and launched into a three-year long drive to re-educate sellers and buyers alike.

The tit-for-tat approach that arose, quite naturally, in the beginning however is a classic example of deterrent based trust where the mutual threat of punishment is offered to generate a motive for consistent behavior to be maintained.

The most famous example of deterrence based trust (DBT) is the stalemate, during the Cold War between the Soviet Union and the US where the concept of Mutually Assured Destruction (MAD for short) coined by John von Neumann who also invented game theory and its mixed-strategy equilibria in two-person zero-sum games. Neumann loves crazy acronyms and MAD filled his requirement of crazy almost instantly.

The concept of MAD as a trust-based mechanism between nations, however, did not originate with Neumann. It had been aired many times before, most notably by the English author Wilkie Collins, writing at the time of the Franco-Prussian War in 1870: "I begin to believe in only one civilizing influence—the discovery one of these days of a destructive agent so terrible that War shall mean annihilation and men's fears will force them to keep the peace", quoting Richard Jordan Gatling who in 1862 patented the Gatling gun in the belief that it would be a weapon to end all wars.

Five years later, in 1867 Alfred Nobel, would present dynamite to the world and say that "The day when two army corps can annihilate each other in one second, all civilized nations, it is to be hoped, will recoil from war and discharge their troops."

Even, Nikola Tesla, whose name crops up in connection with almost everything, had published in 1937 *The Art of Projecting Concentrated Non-dispersive Energy through the Natural Media*, a treatise concerning charged particle beam weapons. Tesla had described his device as a "superweapon that would put an end to all war."

Although a quick channel surf through the news or a look on the web is enough to convince us that war, as a means of interaction between groups of people and nations is far from over the fact that we are still here should be sufficient to convince us that a deterrence-based trust can work within specific contexts to produce a relationship where both parties understand each other's capabilities for destruction and engage in consistent behavior even if they don't really want to.

Deterrence based trust like any other trust model requires communication and three trust-type specific elements shown in figure 3.3

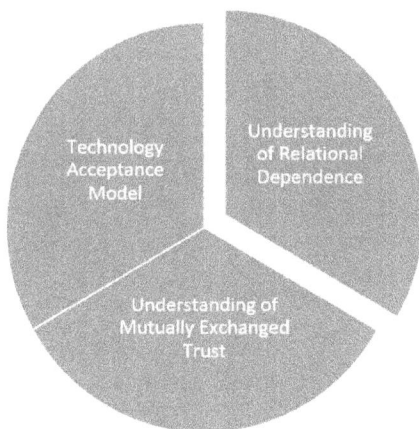

Fig 3.3- *Deterrence-based trust works only when both parties understand the technological capabilities each possesses (which are roughly equal), and each has a clear idea of the degree to which one party is dependent on the other and the benefits the act of giving and receiving trust, in this scenario, offers.*

The DBT approach works well in establishing the initial trust framework in forums or in communal areas (in the real world) where no one party involved has an initial stake. Parks and public streets for instance are kept initially clean because of DBT. Social media platforms like G+ where members can ban and block each other provide a DBT level of initial interaction. Forums where the moderators can instantly ban members who misbehave are another example.

Traditional manager-employee relationships were based on Deterrence Based Trust with the manager being able to fire the employee (stopping them from earning a living) and the employee being able to withhold their labor (preventing the manager from doing their job). Business contracts are another example of Deterrence Based Trust.

As most new relationships start, at this level of trust, all it takes is one violation of expectations or an inconsistency in behavior to destroy the relationship. DBT relationships are cagey, at best. There is never much disclosure at this level because parties are trying to avoid doing anything to sever the relationship before it can develop.

So, depending on your particular scenario:

- Zero Acquaintance Trust needs to be developed when your reputation is not yet strong enough for those you don't know to know something about you.
- Zero Acquaintance Trust measures help form a better perception during initial contact and creates in all parties the confidence necessary to take things forward.
- Deterrence Based Trust helps define boundaries and offers mutual safeguards. Communication is key in how it is received.
- Trust during the Zero Acquaintance stage is extremely fragile. The terms and conditions stipulated by the DTB approach must not just be followed but they must be seen to be followed.

As the eBay example showed Deterrence Based Trust (DBT) should not be the end-all when it comes to building trust. It is a handy way of creating the necessary assurance to initiate contact between two parties with confidence but its zero-sum game nature makes it unnecessarily stressful. There is the implied assumption that throughout a DBT relationship one or both parties will try to find ways to get round the restraints and boundaries that have been created to maximize their gains.

It is important therefore to recognize its limitations and work to get past the initial push-pull dynamic that governs it. In a naturally evolving relationship between two parties, whether they are two people closing a business transaction or two nations that are gradually developing their understanding of each other, Deterrence Based Trust provides sufficient boundaries for better communication to take place and Knowledge Based Trust (KBT) to evolve.

Knowledge Based Trust (KBT)

When there is sufficient contact, over time, what started out as a Deterrence Based Trust relationship that was carefully framed by boundaries and edged with potential punishment now becomes a more equitable and better balanced Knowledge Based Trust (KBT) one.

Knowledge Based Trust takes time to develop (or requires a strong and clear reputation to be possessed by at least one of the parties) and it leads to a clearer calculation of trust assigned because motives, capabilities and reliability can be understood much better. What is more important is since this is a deeper level of trust, infractions do not necessarily break it, immediately because their context can be understood much better.

Most organizational relationships are at this level. The benefits of Knowledge Based Trust are that:

- Trust is not necessarily broken by inconsistent behavior at this level.
- This level relies on information rather than deterrence.

Clear, consistent and honest communication continues to be key here as it does, indeed, with any kind of trust-based relationship. While this is not rocket science the very fact that we are discussing the requirements and itemizing them suggests the difficulty of the task when it comes to implementing it at organizational and even commercial level.

Many large brands and businesses fail to move from the Deterrence Based model of trust they are comfortable with, because they can understand and quantify punitive measures and they can clearly see and measure boundaries and constraints. Their risk-assessment mechanisms are perfectly happy calculating all this and their risk-adverse nature falsely assures them that they have every base covered.

Knowledge Based Trust requires more than relationship building on autopilot based upon the assumption that neither party wants to lose the zero-sum game they're playing. It requires an understanding of the person (or organization) you are dealing with and a deeper appreciation of what motivates their actions. It requires, as a matter of fact the moving of the relationship status between two people, a business and its customers, two rival organizations or even two nations from none to "In a Relationship" (for Facebook fans) knowing full well that what lies ahead, at some point, is going to become a little complicated.

One of the key advantages of Knowledge Based Trust is that in order to work it requires actual knowledge, of the facts that constantly inform the relationship. That makes it less subject to the fluctuations of emotional context and more likely to form a stable base for further development. Because facts are a lot easier to assess and verify than feelings or a sense of potential punishment Knowledge Based Trust can also work at a reputation level where trust is given without direct, prior knowledge or contact with the person or organization.

We can choose to give our trust, as an example, to Amazon or eBay even if we have never used them before because so much is already known about them as a business brand and we are aware of the way they handle disputes and ensure everyone plays fair within their environment. We can choose to give our trust to the doctor checking our vital health signs based on what we know others have shared about him and what those we have talked to in the hospital have told us.

Knowledge Based Trust is an area companies like Google, IBM and Microsoft spend a lot of money researching because it can provide a basis for cognitive computing to operate on and trust to be calculated algorithmically both online and offline. To make matters even more complicated Knowledge Based Trust, as a term is used to refer not just to trust that flows between the boundaries of individuals and institutions, consumers and brands but also to trust that's given amongst colleagues, friends and even work acquaintances who may share a common work environment or a larger work identity. We shall get back to it before this section is out but first we must look at one more application of Knowledge Based Trust.

Of even greater importance than Knowledge Based Trust flowing through the workplace is the kind of Knowledge Based Trust that Google and Microsoft believe can be calculated on the fly creating a handy and truthful evaluation of the authority of a website. While this may seem to be a little futuristic and probably not of any particular concern to us, as individuals or even consumers, nothing could be further from the truth.

We use the web on a daily basis to discover facts, find information, consume news and carry out commercial transactions. In the offline world, whenever we engage in any similar activity we can use a plethora of signals some of which are overt and some of which are subliminal to determine the authority of any source of news, information or goods.

We know, for example, that the TV station that gives us our daily allowance of 30 minutes of news in the evening is an expensive entity to set up. Its buildings, equipment, news tracks and personnel make it difficult to fake and improbable to set up improperly because it will fail quickly and a lot of money will be lost. We also know that it is regulated by the government as it has had to purchase a license for the airwave frequencies it uses and it has competition in other, similar TV stations that also vie for our attention.

All of these observations form a thick layer of verification. While we may accept that the TV station may have a political slant, it is not going to lie outright to us, actively deceive us or try to trick us. And in the unlikely scenario that this very thing happens and our Knowledge Based Trust in the TV station in question is shattered there is an additional layer of Deterrent Based Trust behind it as we know there will be punishment for such behavior meted out by one of the real world recognized authorities (a government watchdog, the judiciary or the police) who themselves have a vested interest in maintaining the flow of trust throughout society so they can function.

The web however, is a decentralized, non-localized world where local authorities operate with difficulty. Its very set up inverts the real world dynamic making it easy to set up and maintain a presence cost-effectively. Within its environment it is easy to create a look that is every bit as convincing as any expensive, authority website and use it to spread misinformation, commit fraud or simply propagate lies.

This is where Knowledge Based Trust comes in. At the moment, websites are deemed to be trustworthy and authorities based upon the number and type of other websites that link to them, the kind of content they put out and the types of people who talk about the content, share it, comment on it and so on. The process is detailed and I wrote an entire book about the change called *Google Semantic Search* where I mentioned that Google's index of the web is moving "from strings to things" understanding objects and people and places and names the same way you and I do.

This is important because a search engine could then also begin to assess credibility based on factual content the same way a person could. Well, better than a person would as a search engine will do it faster, tirelessly and will be able to call up at will the billions of objects and names and places and people (called entities) that it has in its index and cross-reference the interaction between them creating a complex, mini web of connections, each of which is ascribed a numerical value.

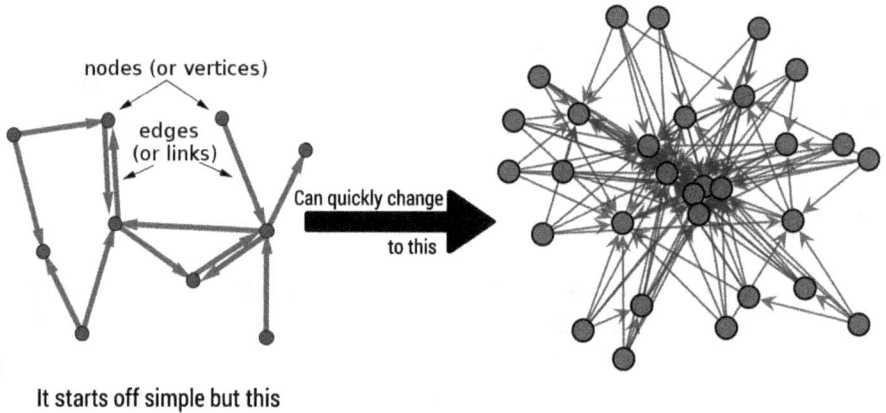

Fig 3.4 – *The numerical value of the relational connections between entities on the web allows the calculation of relative importance each one has and the importance that it then gives to another.*

At present this is a contentious issue the debate about which, paradoxically, is also based on trust or the lack of.

Because the web is becoming larger, denser and more complicated and the divide between the online and offline world is being eroded by the day it is worth actually understanding the issue behind Google's KBT proposal. A paper on the subject, first published in February 2015 is titled: "Knowledge-Based Trust: Estimating the Trustworthiness of Web Sources" and it's authored by eight Googlers, amongst them Xin Luna Dong, a research scientist at Google. The paper begins innocuously enough:

> *"The quality of web sources has been traditionally evaluated using exogenous*

signals such as the hyperlink structure of the graph. We propose a new approach that relies on endogenous signals, namely, the correctness of factual information provided by the source. A source that has few false facts is considered to be trustworthy."

But soon runs into hot water with its suggestion that: "The facts are automatically extracted from each source by information extraction methods commonly used to construct knowledge bases."

Upon publication of the paper there was an article by Hal Hodson published in the *New Scientist* with the title, "Google wants to rank websites based on facts not links" and even searchengineland.com one of the most trustworthy websites for knowledge and facts on search engine optimization ran the headline: "Google Researchers Introduce System To Rank Web Pages On Facts, Not Links".

Now, you might be forgiven for wondering what the fuss is about? Surely a suitably programmed search bot is capable of better ascertaining the truthfulness of facts and determining whether a website is trustworthy or not. But that's exactly that, maybe it is, in most cases but there must be quite a few where it won't be. Facts and how they are determined is a process that is not always straightforward. Given infinite computing power and a suitably large volume of data the problem may be solved, but Google, just like any other business has to work with things in an ergonomic fashion that optimizes the computing power it uses for any given task so that it becomes sustainable.

Under that restriction errors creep in and because errors made by a bot are invisible both to us and to itself, our trust in a bot's ability to understand it has erred and correct it is diminished. It is not beyond possibility to imagine a system that has run amok, errors accumulating on errors and providing wrong answers or branding as untrustworthy websites or entities that are anything but and because it's automated, we have no recourse to setting the record straight.

In a smaller way the plot of the 1985 Terry Gilliam film, *Brazil* is about just such a nightmarish world where the system is simply inhuman and, as a result, inhumane. The perception that we may suddenly be at the mercy of an unwavering bot on a mission, directly affects our trust in the proposed results such a bot would deliver and, by the inevitable halo effect, then taints the trust we are willing to give to a Google branded search that uses such a system.

Two Microsoft researchers by the names of Moritz Y. Becker and Masoud Koleini, working respectively out of the universities of Cambridge and Birmingham, in the UK, thought about that exact vulnerability in our increasingly automated trust-based systems when they authored a paper in 2011 called *Opacity Analysis in Trust Management Systems*. Their contention is that where Opaque Trust Systems are concerned, an unauthorized intruder (or an error) need only get past the system's defenses to then successfully present himself with the full authority of the system it has infiltrated. Their paper suggests some solutions to the problem but it is in the highlighting of something that really needs to be addressed in the very near future that it has its greatest value.

At the moment, Google has not implemented a Knowledge Based Trust approach to search and my guess is it won't until it has solved both how to create transparency in the process from which the answers to search queries based on a fact-assessment system are based and how to allow us enough involvement so we can learn to trust the results. What is of interest to us is that it is lack of trust in the system due to its opacity that currently makes it fail and creates the wave of resistance it has encountered.

The Google researchers were aware of this perhaps. The introduction to their paper begins with a quote from the 17th century English theologian and logician, Isaac Watts, that says: "Learning to trust is one of life's most difficult tasks."

This is the point where we will look at Knowledge Based Trust within the environment of the organization but before we do, Google's momentary failure with an automated system to mine and verify trustworthiness across the web gives us a formula for trust-formation whenever we launch a product or a service that entails cognitive computing of some kind. The kind of product or service that either emulates the working of the human mind or completely replaces it:

- Create transparency in the process
- Allow humans to be able to question the results
- Create a greater symmetry of power in the relationship between humans and the product or the process

Watts, of course, was right. Trusting has to be learnt. Particularly when the trust we require is one that has to take place in the workplace and requires colleagues to trust each other well enough to freely share knowledge.

IBM carried out a detailed study on Knowledge Based Trust that happens within the organization. First, it established that organizations where the people who staff them share knowledge freely because they trust each other and the company they work for, do better in the marketplace, are generally more competitive and, at the same time, manage to be more open, transparent with a greater sense of fulfillment and generally happier employees.

We know by now what happens whenever we look at trust in depth and seek to analyze it. What seems relatively simple devolves into greater complexities, we find ourselves chasing wisps, phantasms, until we are left with what we began with: a quality everyone understands differently and uses similarly, that's dependent on context and culture.

To avoid falling into that trap the IBM researchers created boundaries that allowed them to establish the criteria a knowledge seeker looked for when he considered whether to trust or not the source from which the knowledge came from. Publishing their findings in a paper called: "Trust and knowledge sharing: A critical combination" the IBM researchers discovered that knowledge based trust was further affected by two other types of trust: "…two specific types of trust that are instrumental in the knowledge-sharing process are benevolence-based trust and competence-based trust."

They cited the example of where an employee may feel that a coworker knows the information that the employee needs (competence), but the coworker may not trust that he will be forthcoming at the time when the information is needed (benevolence). Conversely, the employee can be confident that there may be other people who are willing to assist the employee (benevolence), but these people might not possess the knowledge or skills required (competence).

The trustworthiness of a coworker then, according to the study, hinged on a combination of competence-based trust and benevolence-based trust that was calculated through five specific attributes or criteria:

- Common Language
- Common Vision
- Discretion
- Receptivity
- Strong Ties

Attribute	Definition	Significant Impact on Competence-Based Trust	Significant Impact on Benevolence-based Trust
Common Language	The extent to which the knowledge source and seeker communicate clearly sharing a common language	Yes	Yes
Common Vision	The extent a knowledge source and seeker have shared goals, visions and purpose (i.e. are they a team)	Yes	Yes
Discretion	The extent to which the knowledge source is viewed as keeping sensitive source information confidential	No	Yes
Receptivity	The extent to which the knowledge source is a good listener	No	Yes
Strong Ties	The extent to which the knowledge seeker and source converse frequently with each other and have a close relationship	No	Yes

Table 3.1 – *What is notable and what should be evident by now is that despite the fact that we can pinpoint that trust is governed by attributes and can be broken down into types that have a specific effect the stumbling block, each time, or conversely the enabling mechanism is the human ability to communicate clearly, establish connections and form relationships.*

Knowledge Based Trust, in the context that IBM studied it, is interpersonal trust that allows relationships between people belonging to the same group to form so they can function as intended.

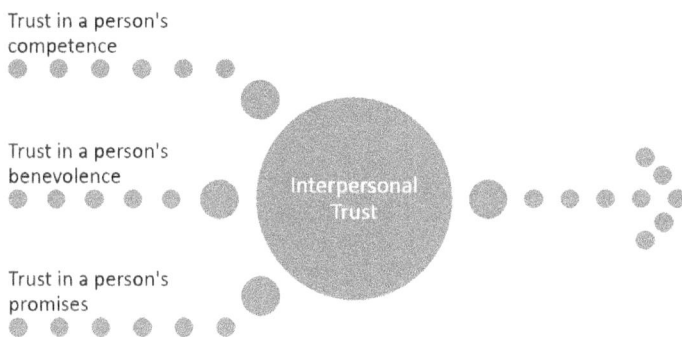

Fig 3.5 - *Interpersonal Trust is formed from Knowledge Based Trust and it is a highly desirable requirement in organizations, the army, tribal groups, social groups, any kind of tightly-knit community.*

The presence of Knowledge Based Trust in organizations gives rise to a high level of interpersonal trust amongst their members and creates cohesive units out of a loose bunch of people. Navy SEAL training at Fort Bragg in North Carolina in the US, puts recruits through such a rigorous training (week six is commonly known as Hell Week) so that they learn to form, quickly the kind of interpersonal trust required for them to act and survive like a unit.

So, depending on your particular scenario:

- Knowledge Based Trust helps you provide an evidence-based approach to building and maintaining trust
- Organization leaders, CEOs, team managers and company owners can benefit from Knowledge Based Trust in their businesses but they must first provide the necessary conditions and boundaries that make it possible (team building, common language, clearly defined goals, a common purpose and an identity of the people within a business)
- Businesses of all types benefit by engendering Knowledge Based Trust and it helps them build their reputation but communication is key to their achieving that goal

Like everything we do in the world trust is an evolving quality, as it accumulates it acquires its own weight of evidence and it morphs. It becomes less fragile, more empowering. It creates assurance where none would exist. Confidence where confidence is needed to make things actually happen. It then becomes the lubricant upon which the gears of the world spin more smoothly and they spin faster.

As we go from the initial moment of Zero Acquaintance where Deterrence Based Trust is required to safeguard us and create, at least, the conditions for a first contact to take place we create better, stronger relationships. These make us feel safer, smarter and stronger. They amplify our own power and safeguard us by removing whatever threat we might have feared existed beforehand.

Not every situation will follow the same trust development arc. Not everyone deserves to have our trust, no matter what. And even where we give our trust and establish relationships that are based on evidence, the Knowledge Based Trust we are prepared to give is different for each person and constantly changing for the same person, over time.

If that were not complex enough to make your head spin we will look at what happens when Knowledge Based Trust, over time, has a sufficient body of evidence to take the relationship we form with another entity (and I use entity here because it can equally well be another person, a brand, a company or – even – a device) for Identification Based Trust (IBT for short) to develop.

Identification Based Trust

Trust, like oxygen, is valuable to us for what it allows us to do. In its presence in human relationships, whether they are personal, professional or any combination of the two flourish. There really is only so much energy to go round. As human beings we don't have infinite physical, mental and psychological resources.

In a low-trust environment a good percentage of those resources are consumed keeping us in play. Like in Machiavelli's world we scheme and plan and second-guess, feint and set up ruses and strategize and get nowhere fast. We take part in zero-sum games (because there is little else you can do in that kind of environment) and win and lose and because it is very difficult to consistently do either, we end up moving forward and backwards incrementally, the gains we make disproportionately small to the effort we've made (think of *The Sopranos* and how little crime pays).

This is why we find it difficult to stand still. We want relationships to constantly evolve so that they take up less time and energy to maintain and deliver greater rewards for a smaller amount of effort. In high-trust environments there is a lot lower friction between individuals. Because we don't have to spend a lot of energy divining a person's motives we are able to better ascertain his capabilities and reliability and work to optimize our relationship with him.

When we are not busy competing we get busy cooperating and then something magical happens. Competition takes away from our strength. It mutually reduces our available energy. It tires us both out until one person 'wins'. Cooperation, however, augments our strengths and minimizes our weaknesses. It allows us to find ways we can work creatively with others so that the gains are maximized for everybody.

Despite the irrefutable logic that leads us from the world of Machiavelli and Hobbes to our own, cooperation still does not come easy and there are good reasons for that. Like any higher-return opportunity the initial investment is also higher and has a greater risk factor. Cooperation requires the establishment and maintenance of Identification Based Trust (IBT).

As the next natural step in the evolution of relationships Identification Based Trust builds on the foundations created by Knowledge Based Trust.

- Identification Based Trust is the highest level of trust you can achieve in a relationship.
- It is achieved when there is an emotional connection between the parties.
- Controls are minimal at this level.
- This is the type of trust that managers and leaders seek in teams.

The trust that develops, after some time, between two people is identification based trust. Special Forces personnel share a special bond that's formed by their shared experiences, that's identification based trust. Companies and businesses that succeed in developing that kind of relationship amongst their staff and with their customers find that the traditional friction-causing barriers have disappeared. Suddenly transactions whether internal (amongst stuff) or external (with customers) become cooperative in nature, both sides wanting the same thing, 'negotiating' the best possible way to achieve it. At that point the "them" and "us" divide disappears.

When traditional antagonists like Google, Apple, Microsoft and Mozilla can come together to work on projects like WebAssembly (also known as wasm), a new binary format, bytecode, that's to be used in browsers in future and promises about 20 times faster performance and loading speeds, it's because they have found ways to create identification based trust amongst them.

When Denise Rousseau, a University Professor at Carnegie Mellon University who holds the H.J. Heinz II Chair in Organizational Behavior and Public Policy, wrote a treatise on the subject for the *Academy of Science Review* she tellingly titled it "Not So Different After All".

She's right. Trust whether between people or organizations stems from the recognition that we cannot do something alone, that success and maybe survival require interdependence. And, as Rousseau herself has said: "Trust is a psychological state comprising the intention to accept vulnerability based upon positive expectations of the intentions or behavior of another."

We place an educated bet on the fact that the other person, organization, institution wants to go on and evolve and succeed and gain, as much as we do. And it's not possible to do it on their own and still make appreciable gains. It's that "available amount of energy" question again. Energy, depending on context, can be anything. Between two neighbors building a fence separating their properties, together, it's the time they have available each weekend to do it. Between two companies it's the know-how of their technical teams and the amount of money they can realistically throw at something and still keep costs reasonable.

Because no one has discovered the gaming equivalent of a cheat code that allows you access to infinite resources, at some point, everyone becomes vulnerable. What happens next depends on how you decide to deal with that vulnerability. It would be awesome for me to be able to tell you that if you establish a Deterrent Based Trust approach in the first instance and then work hard to capture data, analyze it and progress to the Knowledge Based Trust phase, Identification Based Trust is just a step away, you just need to be patient and let it happen.

But that's not how trust works. Despite repeatedly working together many companies cannot get past the "Them" and "Us" stage with other companies, or their customers or even their workers. It takes as much effort to get to the Identification Based Trust of a relationship as it has taken to get to the Knowledge Based Trust stage from zero. Provided you're willing to give it a shot however here's what you need:

- **Clear articulation of common goals and targets.** This is where you define not just your core values and identify the overlap they have with someone else's but also define your larger mission statement and vision. Yes, you both (for instance) may be competing for the same customers in the same environment but both you and your competitor might share a vision of a customer experience that's sterling and a way of working that does not chew up the planet or burn out employees. Working out common ways to make this happen drives up brand equity, brand visibility and employee happiness. It increases market share and drives demand. It helps with customer loyalty and the growth of the business. It is, in other words great for everything except short term goals.

- **A willingness to accept being vulnerable.** The relationship works because both of you need each other. If you cannot admit that, if you hate being dependent and are unwilling to accept the issues that will inevitably arise out of this dependency and work to sort them out, you are unlikely to get the kind of trust you want.

- **A strong sense of empathy.** Whether you are working with colleagues, are forming relationships in your personal life or are thinking about your next big business venture, unless you can develop and exhibit empathy and understanding for the other party you are unlikely to be able to bridge the gap that separates you, sufficiently to make the relationship work.

- **A sense of a shared journey.** It may be difficult to always get to the stage where you share identity. There will always be some differences. What creates a robust relationship at this stage where trust is not compromised despite minimal controls being in place is the sense of a shared journey, shared pressures and a shared goal.

- **Great communication.** If you cannot talk openly, without second guessing the meaning and intent behind each word, you cannot communicate. If you can't communicate there is little chance you will ever get to the Identification Based Trust stage.

What is notable is that there is no formula. While the ingredients are known, each mix will be unique, based on the business cultures and personalities involved. What works in your private life and allows you to enjoy a great relationship with your partner won't work with your colleagues at work and will most probably provide the wrong balance for a mutually beneficial business venture with a competitor.

We have managed to survive this long, as a species, because we constantly find new ways to cooperate. Despite our differences and despite the fact that we all feel the fear of betrayal, we nevertheless make the seemingly irrational choice to admit our vulnerabilities and trust someone.

Two Case Studies and the Swift Trust Theory

Here are two facts that can trip us up: trust requires the forming of a relationship. Relationships take time. There is a real temptation here to use the second fact to forgo the first. If you're in a fast-paced business or are facing a time-critical task, you could argue that there really is no time to form a relationship. Instead of working to earn trust then you could use a different means to jump-start the process you want: fear, threats, rewards, bribes, coercion – you name it, companies of all types and sizes have tried many or all of these.

That's because traditionally trust, in order to emerge, has required the shared history of a group and interaction between its members. Historically, we know that trust requires a long time to form, we learn to trust as we survive the helpless stage of our early years. The time component is inexorable, the relationship one inescapable. But that's trust that rises out of necessity and, one might argue, quite naturally.

What of trust that must happen much faster because businesses really can't wait? Is it unrealistic to expect trust to take place then? Apparently not says Debra Meyerson. She's the Associate Professor of Education and Organizational Behavior and has been looking at the way trust operates in small groups thrown together by circumstances, which have to become quickly operational without having the luxury to wait it out for time to pass and relationships to form.

These groups, whether they are in the army or business display certain characteristics that we can extract and use in many other situations. These temporary work groups are typically formed in order to accomplish a specific, often complex and critical project through the collaboration of specialists who possess very different but interdependent skills. These experts may have little opportunity to get to know each other in advance of the project. Nor do they know if they will be working together again after the project is completed.

Despite the fact that their histories preclude trust, research analysis has shown that trust is paradoxically present in these situations. One reason for this, believes, Meyerson, lies in the fact that they are assigned specific roles on the team and by referring to such roles everybody knows fairly well what is expected of them and what they can expect of others. Accordingly, Meyerson notes that 'an increase in role clarity leads to a decrease in expected ill will, and an increase in trust presumes that roles in temporary systems are clear'.

So communication, clarity of purpose and a shared mission are established pretty quickly and then the subsequent call to action and clearly described boundaries within which every member of a team has to act, seem to seal the deal. But that sounds a little too simple, when it can take months or years for trust to emerge in other scenarios where these same ingredients are also present, the fact that these groups enjoy it so quickly suggests something more is required.

It's an ingredient that another trust researcher, Guido Möllering, currently professor of Professor of Organization and Management at the Jacobs University, in Bremen, Germany, has been looking at for some time. Möllering is also fascinated by the way trust emerges quickly in ad hoc groups and he has used the work of another German, the sociologist, Georg Simmel to draw attention to what he believes is the missing ingredient that makes trust emerge swiftly, when rational thought says it shouldn't.

In his 2006 book, aptly titled *Trust Beyond Risk: the Leap of Faith* Möllering quotes Simmel: "Without the general trust that people have in each other, society itself would disintegrate, for very few relationships are based entirely upon what is known with certainty about another person, and very few relationships would endure if trust were not as strong as, or stronger than, rational proof or personal observation." He then goes on to show that the missing ingredient that actually makes trust emerge is a willing suspension of distrust.

There is reason in his argument. Just as light appears as the absence of darkness, the moment distrust is consciously overruled a tentative measure of trust emerges spontaneously. Giving someone "a chance", "the benefit of the doubt", "an opportunity to prove themselves", are all instances of the willing suspension of distrust.

Meyerson has shown that in the teams she studied, team members tend not to commit themselves too much in the beginning and remain more cautious than they appear. They follow the 'principle of gradualness' where they wade into trust but let direct experience guide them who to eventually truly trust within the team. The reason there is a willingness to suspend critical judgment at the beginning is found in both social and cognitive mechanisms that create a norm, within the context of the group.

What of business? How is research done in small temporary group settings, tasked with an urgent task, relate to our buying a bagel from a street vendor? Entering the premises of an out of the way bric-a-brac shop, or doing business with a fruit stall vendor by the side of the road?

Look at the five points needed to get from Knowledge Based Trust to Identification Based trust, again:

- Clear articulation of common goals and targets.
- A willingness to accept being vulnerable.
- A strong sense of empathy.
- A sense of a shared journey.
- Great communication.

Add to them two more supplied by Möllering:

- Social context
- Cognitive analysis

A food vendor in NYC enjoys an entirely different level of social trust than a similar food vendor in, let's say, downtown Istanbul. There is the perception of the entire culture with its checks, controls and balances, behind it, that makes the difference.

Similarly, our visual inspection and analysis of the entire set up of the vendor plays a key role in our decision of whether we are willing to suspend distrust and take a chance. A bagel stand that is visibly dirty, looks ill-maintained and a vendor in unwashed attire will affect our choice immediately in either setting. Our willingness to suspend distrust is logically predicated on the absence of logical reasons to distrust.

I often use myself as a guinea pig as I travel around the globe, observing not just how others interact with me when they know nothing about me but also how I make choices when I am cut off from my own social group, my own language and – often – my own culture.

As you come off the EU terminal at Frankfurt Airport to go to the waiting area for Transatlantic flights the first thing you see on the left hand side as you come off the ramp is Hebere's, a traditional German bakery that serves, alongside fresh bread, sandwiches, and sweets. As it is the very first thing you come across you'd think it's situated at a prime spot, but the bakery works under extremely difficult conditions: Being in an airport it has an international clientele that is usually one-off. No word of mouth publicity. No reputation. No repeat business. It also faces stiff competition from adjoining coffee and pub places, the bakery does not sell coffee or any alcoholic beverage, both of which are big attractions for weary travelers. It stupidly does not even have a wi-fi that's free with purchase (though I did find a connection but they would not give me the password to).

To solve the problem Hebere's applies the one thing none of its competitors can (or do): Transparency. Quite literally. Apart from the oven that does the baking everything else is behind clear glass.

You can watch the food that is to be baked or the food you are to buy being prepared if you want, for as long as you want. A baker stands, artfully creating bread shapes to go in the oven, the dough in his hygienically gloved hands, quite atavistic in the connection it creates in our minds.

The selling area is also open to observation. The front of the bakery is all glass. The display is meticulous, the lighting chosen with care. On this score, nothing has been left to chance. By being so radically transparent the bakery does the impossible: it stops the passersby eye long enough for the message of trust (and dare I say, authenticity) fostered by its radical transparency, to work on them.

Having two hours to kill before a flight to the US I stood watching as one after the other of the busy people passing by stopped, looked, went on to make a purchase. They totally ignored two pubs and a cafe within thirty yards from it and all because the bakery applied every single one of the seven points of swift trust we've detailed.

Swift trust is a paradox even within the greater paradox of trust itself. Arising spontaneously as a result of the willingness to consciously suspend distrust it is also incredibly fragile. All it takes is a violation of one of the necessary conditions that help it arise, for it to completely evaporate. And such violations, experience has shown are still not very difficult to come by in our times.

Fig 3.6 – *Hebere's in Frankfurt Airport put their entire operation under glass, arresting the eye and starting a 'conversation' that convinces the traveler to willingly suspend distrust and take a chance on them.*

On the island of Lefkas, in Greece, where I occasionally spend a few weeks each summer a transformation has taken place. With tourism being the island's main industry there is tremendous pressure for businesses to make enough money in the summer to last them through the lean winter months.

As you can imagine the competition is fierce and one eating place, from the outside, looks pretty much like another, just as one boat ride looks much like another. This is why the business owners have taken advantage of Trip Advisor reviews. With most restaurants and tourist attractions on the island sporting a Trip Advisor sign, discovering the quality of each is only a couple of smartphone swipes away.

Not everyone however has moved with the times.

The reason I took the photograph in Fig 3.7 is that this place basically uses a traditional outbound marketing campaign. In a street crowded with restaurants, each of which tries to create a welcoming atmosphere that will entice the visitors to come in, this one has chosen to simply yell loudest that it's the best place to get gyros, in town.

The self-proclamation of "best gyros in town" should, of course, be taken with a pinch of salt (we could hardly expect them to say "we do the same mediocre food you can find everywhere else").

Fig 3.7 - *This is an eating place in Lefkada (one of the Greek holiday islands I stayed at). It is on the main street of Nydri (one of its main villages). The main street is lined with eating places, most of them offering traditional Greek food called Gyros (lamb which is where the Gyros part comes in – cooked vertically and sliced in thin shavings and served wrapped in pita bread). Tourists go up and down the main street which becomes pedestrianized between the hours of 9.00pm and 2.00am. (all shops are open at that time, including supermarkets, butcher shops, bakeries, ice-cream parlors, foot massage places and restaurants and bars) and they decide where to go for dinner based on look and feel.*

Although it looks busy (the picture was taken around 11.00pm when each restaurant is at peak capacity) it really isn't. As offline consumers we have become sophisticated enough to now expect more social proof than the self-proclamation of greatness in what someone has to offer. Most of the competitors of the restaurant in Fig 3.7 have Trip Advisor ratings which they display prominently and, as a result, are so busy you will not get a table unless you turn up a little earlier or simply book beforehand.

These two examples could not be further apart. Both Hebere's and the Gyros restaurant in Lefkas do the exact same thing: they both tell us how great they are and that we should trust them and give them our business. They each do it very differently.

Hebere's chooses to lay itself open, accepting vulnerability, opening up every part of its business to our gaze and then using the bread preparation area as an additional point of attraction by showing off not just skill in the making of bread and pizza dough, but also artistry. The Gyros restaurant in Lefkas expects us to take it entirely on faith and believe their word. It is easy to see which of the two benefits from the swift trust that arises, and which doesn't.

Summary

The more we look into what trust is and how it works the more it seems to vanish from our eyes, breaking up into a myriad different pieces, each governed by specific conditions. Researchers on the subject should really be called trustonauts, their findings documented, at times, like those of the blind men and the elephant. Taken together though, they begin to add up to a granular picture where trust is always subject to the four step sequence of:

- Contact
- Perception
- Assessment
- Connection

Trust, we have seen in this chapter, is really a developmental quality that has a starting point (and conditions) which become part of a relationship. It can be developed further from there but not without work. Whether trust happens slowly, over time, or swiftly over a handshake, an ad promotion, or a shared name and telephone number, it depends upon the perception of humanity and the willingness to express vulnerability.

In moving forward we shall examine further some of the key applications of trust in a modern setting and some of its many variations. We shall see just what exactly is meant by "work" when it comes to trust (and relationships) and what it is that we can learn from all this so we actually behave and act in a more trustworthy manner.

Five Key Questions to Answer

1. Where do you think your organization, or your relationships stand in the three developmental stages of trust from Deterrence Based to Knowledge Based to Identification Based Trust?
2. Knowing what you do now, is there something you would change

about your work environment, your style of leadership or your approach to business deals and partnerships? Give a detailed explanation.

3. How does your business (or how do you) act to elicit Swift Trust?

4. How do you (your organization or your business) show you are vulnerable?

5. How trustworthy do you think you appear to those who don't know anything about you?

4

The Five Flavors of Trust

If trust is such a fundamental force in our lives that we all feel it even if we can't always articulate it, then it should be easy to define in particular settings. Researchers say both "yes" and "no" to this. Trust is, indeed, so fundamental that it morphs in qualities in every situation and even within situations where it has been precisely established and clearly been defined, it manages to slip through the cracks formed by human connections and mutate yet again. In this chapter we are going to look at some of the different 'flavors' of trust, analyze them and see what it is that makes them tick and what we can learn from them. The primary issue is learning where and how to apply some of the things we learn in a way that makes work more rewarding and working relationship more efficient and, maybe even, trustworthy.

Since 2012 global happiness has become a quality we measure and there is an organization that uses a variety of factors to rank the world's nations on what I suppose we can call a Happiness Index. "The aspiration of society is the flourishing of its members," said Jeffrey Sachs, Director of the Earth Institute, Columbia University. "This report gives evidence on how to achieve societal well-being. It's not by money alone, but also by fairness, honesty, trust, and good health. The evidence here will be useful to all countries as they pursue the new Sustainable Development Goals."

The report, produced by the Sustainable Development Solutions Network (SDSN), contains analysis from leading experts in the fields of economics, neuroscience, national statistics, and describes how measurements of subjective well-being can be used effectively to assess national progress.

Denmark, was the happiest nation in the world according to the 2014 report and, as a country, it has been topping the list for some time. The Danes have ranked high among the happiest nations in the world. In 2014 they occupied the top spot and in 2015 they were still amongst the world's five happiest nations. Research indicates this is because Danes have a high level of trust, even for people they don't know. Apparently, trust makes people happy. Happy people behave differently and their behavior, taken cumulatively, affects the entire social fabric and culture of their country.

Trust and happiness? Related and affecting each other? As if trust was not hard enough to define and then measure, happiness had to also be added to the mix. From a practical research point of view we may as well start asking for a newt's eye and the blood of a freshly killed baby bat as the secret ingredients we need to make our marketing efforts work and trust happen.

Yet the data shows the connection. America, which has never been amongst the world's happiest nations is also experiencing a drain in trust:

"You can take our word for it. Americans don't trust each other anymore." Begins an Associated Press report, "We're not talking about the loss of faith in big institutions such as the government, the church or Wall Street, which fluctuates with events. For four decades, a gut-level ingredient of democracy — trust in the other fellow — has been quietly draining away."

In 2013 Associated Press worked with GfK, the global marketing and research firm, to poll Americans on how they felt about their fellow citizens. The results were unsettling. Americans, it appeared, are suspicious of each other in everyday encounters. "…only one-third of Americans say most people can be trusted. Half felt that way in 1972, when the General Social Survey first asked the question."

That's a significant decline and it affects not just nations but also organizations. Not just staff working within them, but also their customers. In my last real job I worked for the John Lewis Partnership in the UK in a communication capacity. John Lewis is a leading retail department store that also owns the upmarket supermarket chain of Waitrose. It is staff-owned, internally governed by a two-tier staff-participatory, governance-by-committee system that sounds crazy to any conventional business but which its staff make work but what is most important here is that its internal mission statement is "To make its customers and staff happy".

In 2013, following the backlash over its corporation tax bill, Amazon (which had been topping the popularity polls) fell to fourth place and John Lewis became the UK's most trusted brand. While the brand is strictly national and has not yet expanded beyond the UK borders it's by no means a lightweight. Its 2014 annual report shows revenue of $15.5 billion.

By topping the list of more than 100 brands, beating global rivals such as Amazon and Virgin, John Lewis earned *The Guardian* newspaper's headlines praise for building "trust capital" and was featured in the UK's *Retail Gazette* as one of the most "human" brands as defined by the Human Era Index report. The Human Era Index report, which dishes out scores of 1-10 based on whether companies are trustworthy, honest and caring to its customers, quantified thousands of customers' experiences across 1,000+ brands before it awarded John Lewis a high mark of 8.8.

In the next chapter, as we begin to look at the components of loyalty and figure out where trust belongs in them, the John Lewis story will become even more important. For now, however, consider that this is how much the world has changed. We're looking at nations and businesses and institutions, judging them not like the complex, behemoths they appear to be. Not like the infallible, perpetual motion machines they would like us to think they are, grinding slowly but inevitably and deserving unquestionable loyalty, respect and obedience. We judge them the way we judge people. We want them to be trustworthy. To be happy. We want them to trust us, and when they have contact with us (or we with them) we want them to make us happy (or, at the very least not give us reasons to be unhappy).

The human qualities that become the connecting threads of our relationships: vulnerability, interdependence, loyalty, love, trust and happiness, are now the key requirements for any relationship to work, all relationships without exception. We cut no slack to any of them just because they are big, complicated, seemingly vital. All of these institutions, businesses and even nations are made of people.

People bring in their qualities to the places they live in and the places they work in. Businesses, communities, villages, cities and countries then become what their people eventually make them. While this may sound a little utopian as a point of view and disregard the fact that companies and villages, communities and countries already have a culture that's part of their history and that culture changes slowly and only after much effort, the fact remains that human qualities transcend even the most intransigent conditions.

The annals of war, for instance, are full of countless instances where the human spirit has simply shone through. They range from German and Russian troops fighting it out in the Kovno-Wilna-Minsk region, stopping and signing a temporary truce to stand side-by-side and battle it out with a megapack of starved out wolves to the unknown WWII Japanese Officer who risked everything to give a Notre Dame sports ring back to Mario "Motts" Tonelli. Tonelli was a soldier in the U.S. Army and a former college football star who had played football for the Fighting Irish and in 1937 even made an awe-inspiring 70-yard run in the fourth quarter against USC to set his team up for the winning touchdown, which he also scored. The ring held immense sentimental value to him.

Of all the ones that could exemplify the moment humanity shines through despite it being tightly wound in constraints that demand it not be shown, the one instance that stands above them all is a classic bomber-in-trouble war story. During WWII Charles Brown, a B-17 bomber pilot on his return from a bombing raid over Germany in December 1943 run into a sudden attack that wounded half of his crew and left their plane virtually defenseless over enemy territory.

As Brown attempted to maintain control of the aircraft, he took a quick glance out the window. To his dismay, he saw a German Messerschmitt piloted by 2nd Lt. Franz Stigler, an ace fighter out on an extended revenge spree to avenge his brother August, who had been killed early in the war by American pilots. Resigned to his fate, Brown looked his would-be executioner in the eyes. To his surprise, the German gave Brown a friendly nod and escorted his aircraft to safety.

Many years later Franz Stigler would explain that when he first saw the

B-17 engine sputtering over his airbase, he had every vengeful intention of putting it to the ground, but when he maneuvered his plane for the kill shot, it became apparent that Brown and his crew were incapable of putting up any resistance. Their plane was riddled with holes, their gunner was dead and the survivors were all huddled in the hull tending to their wounds.

To Stigler, to kill them wouldn't only be unfair; it would be equal to murder, which was unacceptable for the German pilot who lived by the warrior code of honor. And so, he began to fly in formation with the bomber, tricking German anti-air crews below into thinking that it was one of their own captured B-17s. He did this until they reached the North Sea, at which point Stigler gave the grateful Americans one last salute and returned back to base. Brown eventually landed safely in Allied territory.

Forty years later, the two pilots would miraculously find each other and actually and become the best of friends, calling each other brothers and even going on numerous fishing trips together. And all because in 1943, Stigler remembered the words of one of his commanding officers, who said, "You fight by rules to keep your humanity."

It is humanity that's actually propagated through the gossamer, reaching tendrils of trust and the emergence of happiness. In the 21st century we don't want to do business with impersonal, faceless entities, government bureaucracies or nations that have no human face. We have now come to expect that they humanize themselves, learn to respond to us in a language we can understand and strive to earn our trust and gain our confidence in them.

The nations topping the Happy Index in 2015 were:

1. Switzerland
2. Iceland
3. Denmark
4. Norway
5. Canada

Canada seems an aberration, an English-speaking nation in a bevy that's dominated by the Nordic group. *The Economist* spotted this as well and ran an analysis on the subject concluding that:

"The combination of geography and history has provided Nordic governments with two powerful resources: trust in strangers and belief in individual rights. A Eurobarometer survey of broad social trust (as opposed to trust in immediate family) showed the Nordics in leading positions. Economists say that high levels of trust result in lower transaction costs—there is no need to resort to American-style lawsuits or Italian-style quid-pro-quo deals in order to get things done. But its virtues go beyond that. Trust means that high-quality people join the civil service. Citizens pay their taxes and play by the rules. Government decisions are widely accepted."

Trust then acts indeed like a lubricant that allows the complex machinery of society to function properly. Remove it from the equation and the friction caused is so high that things begin to crumble.

Yet, in every situation, trust can be almost magically captured, reverse-engineered and analyzed, its components rendered bare for us to see. Do you want to have a successful business customers love to give money to? Do you want to live in a country where things just work, the country is a safe environment and everyone is happy being there? Do you crave to be the kind of guy that people line up to get to know? Talk to? Do business with? Would you love to be in a relationship where "working on it" simply does not feel like work?

These are massively different things separated by categories into Professional, Aspirational, Personal. Yet they are all subject to the same dynamic that arises out of these 'secret' ingredients:

- Be sincere
- Be honest
- Be transparent
- Be consistent
- Be thoughtful
- Be human

It's hardly magic, let alone rocket science. The question of why we find it so difficult to be like this is answered by the emotions that push us to the opposite spectrum of behavior: insecurity and fear. Companies and brands (just like people) are insecure about who they are, how strong they are and whether anyone will really like them. They are afraid of failure, afraid they will say the wrong thing. So they spend a lot of time and energy crafting 'messages' starting campaigns, creating opportunities to impress us. If you think how is it possible for them to behave that way when they are large companies with a lot of staff and coffers full of money, consider how we behave when puberty strikes and we get in our teens and all we can think about is the opposite sex. Tunnel-vision and a narrow focus, rarely helps anyone behave right.

In the sections that follow we look at trust arising in five distinct environments, each representing a huge and sometimes overlapping segment of our modern world:

- Commercial
- Operational
- Algorithmic
- Interpersonal
- Personal

Commercial Trust

A McKinsey Report from 2011 shows that the global digital economy is bigger than that of Spain which according to *Trading Economics*, in 2011, was worth $1,431 billion in US dollars and the world's 14th largest economy. An even more recent study by *Accenture and Oxford Economics* suggests that the increased use of digital technologies could add almost as much again: $1.36 trillion to the total global economic output in 2020.

With that kind of money at stake you'd think the way to establish commercial trust on the web will be a clearly understood process governed by very precise steps. Well this is not quite so. As a matter of fact because commerce is about as old as our notion of trust when we critically examine the first, to look for the second we very much get a situation of now you see it, now you don't.

> "…I maintain that trust is irrelevant to commercial exchange and that reference to trust in this connection promotes confusion."

So says Oliver Williamson in his hugely influential book *The Mechanisms of Governance*. By drawing attention at a high theoretical level to equivalences and differences between market and non-market decision-making, management and service provision, Williamson was influential in the 1980s and 1990s debates on the boundaries between the public and private sectors and he was awarded the Nobel Memorial Prize in Economic Sciences for it, in 2009.

Still, even Nobel Laureates are not infallible and Williamson is no exception. Williamson has expertly analyzed and offered a precise mechanism for the field of Transactional Cost Economics (TCE), the complex negotiating steps that take two parties from what now know to be the Zero Acquaintance stage to a manageable, working relationship. However he has an approach to institutional trust that is very much part of the problem many of us see with what was going on in the world of business in the last century.

Williamson's economist-trained mind struggles with trust as a human trait that forever changes. He craves the stability of calculated outcomes based on specific risk-assessment probabilities that every rations business needs, and we feel for him.

In the 20th century the challenge was to understand institutions and organizations. To get a grip on behavior that had to be rooted in rationality and to establish workable boundaries in order to define that world. The world we have now left behind. Transactional Cost Economics seemed to offer an easy in.

Transaction Costs Economics (TCE) use transactions as the basic unit of analysis to quantify inter-organizational relationships. It is generally recognized that TCE is at the heart of the new institutional theory of organizations. Another Nobel Laureate, Douglass North, would back this up further, writing in his book, *Institutions, Institutional Change, and Economic Performance* in 1990 that "…in the model of a perfect market, transactions are both costless and instantaneous. Transaction costs tend to be zero if information is perfect and symmetrical among parties."

The cost of information, in that model, both changes the cost-efficiency of the transaction and affects the symmetry of the relationship. Armed with the power of hindsight we could argue that the information in question is reputation. That the symmetry of information held by each party is an understanding of motives, but that is semantics in the linguistic sense of the word. We're splitting hairs because the big picture TCE specialists like Williamson and North study is different to the one we are looking at today, when information costs virtually nothing to acquire, share and propagate. Transaction Cost Economics is no longer governed by it.

Williamson and North distrust trust as a notion because it makes their jobs harder. Indeed Williamson goes on as far as to say in his 1985 book, *The Economic Institutions of Capitalism*:

> *"It is redundant at best and can be misleading to use the term 'trust' to describe commercial exchange for which cost-effective safeguards have been devised in support of more efficient exchange. Calculative trust is a contradiction in terms'"*

Reading his work we can only marvel at the general willingness to accept institutions and organizations as perfectly rational actors exhibiting highly logical behavior. In Williamson's worldview we assume that organizations would obey the transactional requirements established by what we would now call Deterrence-Based Trust and not try to cheat to 'win', even when there is no hope of seeing any benefits in developing the relationship further.

Williamson and North are not really there to help us understand how a brand gains loyal customers or how a business increases its market share. Theirs is not the challenge of how to humanize a business that may straddle 11 countries and three continents, have a workforce on tens of thousands of employees and dance to the traditional capitalist tune of "maximize shareholder value" at any cost. They are there to help establish the rational boundaries within which two parties, both of which are driven by a self-serving motive for gain that Machiavelli and Hobbes would find intimately familiar, can establish sufficient ground to work well together.

That there are holes in the TCE theory and its strict calculus-based Transactional Cost Economics is evidenced by the fact that both Williamson and North need to engage in mental gymnastics to make their approach fit every situation. Faced with specific examples drawn from their writings both men contort the idea of information and knowledge to make it behave in the role that now trust and reputation are being called upon to perform.

In his critique of this in his 2011 book *The Moral Foundation of Economic Behavior*, David Rose who's Professor of Economics at the Department of Economics at the University of Missouri-St. Louis writes:

> *"Although it is true that institutions solve many of the same problems that trust solves this does not demonstrate that the ability to genuinely trust*

others is superfluous. Could one not argue that guns are superfluous because spears have demonstrated an ability to kill an enemy?"

We don't have to look far to see the impact the absence of trust in institutional bodies plays. The Libor (London Interbank Offered Rate) scandal which mired some of the biggest banks in fraud litigation, Enron, Lehman Brothers and the VW toxic emissions scandal are all instances where an institution or an entire industry used self-appointed credentials to police itself under the premise that they could be trusted.

History is rich with instances where evidently the institutional transactional safeguards Williamson and North propose were insufficient to make up for the absence of trust. When we each now have, at the level of the individual, the acquired knowledge and expertise necessary to assess any institution, individual, business or organization and the ability to obtain the necessary information, purely calculative approaches to the transaction in the manner suggested by Transactional Cost Economics, simply doesn't work, or at least it doesn't work well enough to make a business viable in the long term.

Quality of
Information

Good
Online
Experience

Security

Perceived
Risk

Online
Trust

Brand
reputation

Fig 4.1 – *All of the elements that go into generating trust in a remote, mostly asynchronous online transaction revolve around the ability of the individual to obtain and assess the necessary information and decide on his own.*

Writing in *The Journal of Electronic Commerce* just after the turn of the millennium Harrison McKnight, Associate Professor in Accounting and Information Systems, and Norman Chervany from the Carlson School of

Management, nailed the scope of the challenge when they wrote in their introduction to an article on trust in eCommerce:

> *"To many consumers, e-commerce represents an excursion beyond the unknown into the unknowable. A generation ago, purchasing drugs or dry goods from the corner store or dealing with a lawyer or doctor involved a known quantity. One could inspect the goods and evaluate the vendor before making the purchase. The druggist and the family doctor and the neighborhood lawyer, like their clients, had been there for many years. Clients knew them by reputation through trusted friends and by their own personal experience with them as professionals and as members of a club or church or PTA."*

The "unknowable" which in 2002, when the article first appeared was just beginning to become a thing, is now all around us. We can make one-click purchases from the cell phones in our pockets, on the move. We can use our tablets to research and buy stuff while in bed or for the 35% of people who according to a Staples survey use their tablets in the bathroom, while they're on the can.

How trust is formed in an environment that is as empowering as the web of today, in all its forms, is a story of the transition from the known to the unknowable only to find that the secret key needed was something we had known all along: information, reputation and relationships.

Trust in the digital environment requires:

- Perceived risk
- Good online experience
- Quality of information
- Word of mouth
- Security
- Brand reputation

None of these six elements can exist independently of each other or work on its own. A partial presence of them signals failure to understand what's needed. Which means failure to create any kind of trust.

Suppose, just for a moment, that we had the perfect online customer in someone who has a credit card, cash to burn and is looking to make a purchase. This ideal, highly motivated online customer then lands on the dream website.

While the website he is on is one he's never heard of before, the layout, product description, product visuals, ease of navigation and color scheme, all work to make him feel at ease.

He knows instantly that he is in the hands of professionals. He begins to click around and the website experience is excellent. The navigation makes sense. He can easily find out more information about the product he wants to buy (and even watch a video about it), the pictures are of high quality, the calls to action clear and logical. As a matter of fact the entire online experience is exactly how he'd want it to be in real life if there was a perfect shop assistant ready to serve him the moment he walked in the store.

Impressed by the quality of information and the pleasantness of the experience he wonders why he hasn't heard of the website before and decides to ask a couple of his friends. Imagine his surprise and pleasure at hearing some great testimonial directly from them. The website is reliable, the goods came fast. The transaction was uneventful.

He's convinced. He feels good about himself and his choice. He is about to proceed to checkout when he wonders about security. After all he's about to use his credit card, inputting the details in a website he's never used before. That too is covered however. The website has easy to find information for first-time purchasers that explains the process, lets them know who will process the payment and whether the credit card details are kept on record or not.

Being diligent, this ideal customer, also does one more, specific Google search before purchase. He wants to see reviews of other people who have used this particular website. A few hundred pages come up. Ranging from forum posts to articles to individual reviews, one glowing story after another sing the website's praises, not just in terms of products bought and goods sold, but also about its rags-to-riches story, how it came into being as an idea and its owners struggled to make it what it is today. He discovers that the company behind it is active in community services, helping keep its local areas clean and plating trees in the park. Helping homeless shelters by donating blankets and maintaining a summer intern program.

It would now take a pack of wild dogs foaming at the mouth and the Zombie Apocalypse happening at the same time to stop this ideal customer from jumping at the chance to throw his money and add his custom to the website's list of satisfied customers.

In addition he would feel so good with his purchase that he'd be dying to tell all his friends about it. The experience would have made him feel so good that, a true evangelist for the business, he'd only want that feeling to be shared by others.

Trust never came up at any step in this sequence of events. And that's just it about trust as a whole. If we need to discuss it specifically in the context of a relational transaction, there clearly is a problem.

Operational Trust

The best definition of Operational Trust I came across was given by Major Nicole Blatt, USAF when for the 9th International Command and Control Research and Technology Symposium Coalition Transformation she submitted a paper titled *Operational Trust: A New Look at the Human Requirement in Network Centric Warfare*. Working from the point of view of a battlefield unit, needing to work cooperatively with her own and allied forces on a large scale battlefield Blatt wrote: "Trust is a bet that those entities, which you cannot control, will act in a predictable manner that is favorable to your cause." And she went on to specify operational trust as "trust in the information, subordinates, superiors, peers, and equipment."

In that last sentence she describes a universe. Whether you are an army or a warehouse supplier. A force of Marines operating remotely in a battlefield that itself is made up of many other moving pieces, or one of Amazon's fulfillment centers charged with getting items purchased to an address in time for a birthday party, the challenge, from a logistics point of view is the same: You need to be able to trust the process. Trust in the process means it is dependable. Dependable processes deliver consistent quality. Consistent quality leads to predictable results and end user loyalty.

What is notable here is that the military, which gave business its traditional command-and-control, top-down structure, the same military that became the hierarchical model for corporations, has morphed and changed, ahead of them.

In the 21st century the military is looking stripped down, flatter in its command structure with entrepreneurial-style autonomy and initiative being exercised by its armed units in the field. It has become leaner, smarter and more responsive than ever before while many of the businesses being set up today still operate under assumptions of command lines and corporate control that are neither accurate nor reflective of the fluidity of the situations they operate in. Many businesses could benefit by relearning the lessons of intelligent units and lateral communication that modern armies have learnt so well.

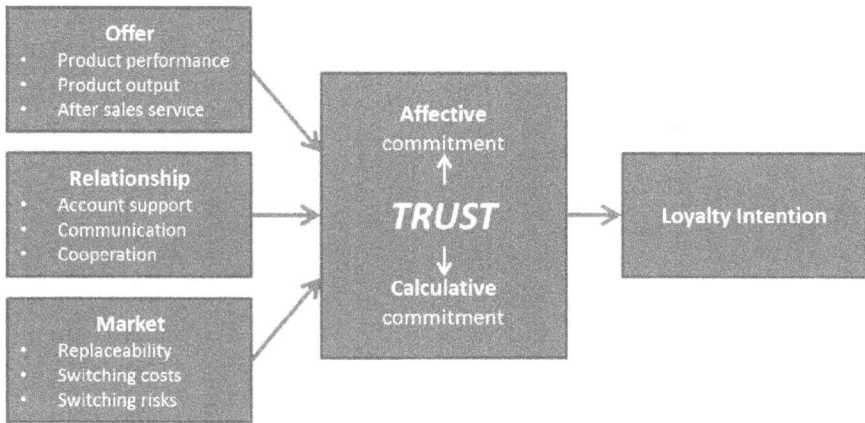

Fig 4.2 – *Operational Trust comes out of three distinct steps comprised of the Offer, the Relationship that is formed based on the service available and the Market that's created through mitigation of costs. The trust that's developed is both calculative (per Oliver Williamson mode) and affective (engendering an emotional response). The end result is loyalty.*

Operational Trust is comprised of three distinct steps:

- Offer
- Relationship
- Market

Each one, as shown in Fig 4.2 is made up of a further three steps. Whether we are talking battlefield processes or warehouse fulfillment center or department store supply chain here is immaterial. The labels may change a little but the ingredients are the same.

If the operational trust exists, if the ingredients that make up the Offer-Relationship-Market approach are true, then we get Williamson's and

North's calculative commitment appearing as if from nowhere and, because we really cannot give out trust in anything, consistently without actually feeling something for it and the people behind it, we also get affective commitment where we humanize the product and the company behind it and make it part of our lives. This is why soldiers name their guns and people form relationships with (and give names to) their cars.

In what is a bugle call of alarm Henry Mintzberg, the Cleghorn professor of management studies at McGill University in Montreal, wrote an article in Canada's *Globe and Mail* where he ascribed the loss of operational trust to the short-termism plaguing many modern companies in the 21st century.

He cited a string of examples including Chevrolet and its ignition problem that resulted in 147 deaths, Toyota and its Takata airbag problem. Goldman Sachs and its alleged manipulation of the market for recycled aluminum. VW and its vehicle emissions fraud as evidence that the phenomenon was more widespread, its causes rooted in our cultures and spread through very similar approaches. The overt focus of goals upon immediate, short-term gains to the exclusion of almost everything else.

The artisans, craftsmen and stall holders who, across time, sold their wares from a stall or from under a tarpaulin in the medieval village square, understood operational trust. They knew that the market share they craved that would make them famous, successful and wealthy, that would in short, ensure their survival, came only with pride in their work and the assurance that their name would stand for unimpeachable quality.

Living examples of the approach are the Italian gun manufacture Beretta which has operated since at least 1526 and the cymbal maker Zildjian that was founded in 1623 in Turkey. In Japan where the culture of honor has traditionally always been closely tied to pride in the quality of one's work, there is a sake brewery called Sudo Honke that was established in 1141 AD and a hot-spring hotel called Nisiyama Onsen Keiunkan, which has existed since the year 705 AD. The John Lewis Partnership, in the UK at more than 150 years old is a mere youngster when compared to these seemingly immortal companies.

Operational trust as Blatt concludes in her paper is "The aggregate trust that is required by every person to orchestrate and accomplish a campaign or endeavor."

In our times this also requires:

- Clear communication within the organization
- Alignment of values within the company
- Alignment of company values and customer expectations
- Consistency of message at the customer interface
- A willingness to stand behind the brand promise

Given how trust, once clearly defined and bounded can be estimated to some degree it seems reasonable that we could get machines to do it for us in at least some environments and situations. That's exactly the notion behind algorithmic trust, which we examine next.

Algorithmic Trust

Trust is a human quality so the primary question when it comes to algorithmic trust is whether it is even a feasibility. Yet, we live in a time of ever intelligent programming and ever more cognitive capable machines. As research progresses we realize that much of our uniqueness may not be so unique after all. As human beings we are prone to behavioral patterns and repetitive behavior which we conveniently neither notice nor remember for very long if we do. Our lives therefore appear full of wonder, excitement and the unexpected, even when they really are not.

This prevents our minds from shutting down with boredom and our brains from overloading and burning out with constant activity. Our cognitive lives, in other words are the result of a process of cognitive optimization that is a wonder in itself, not least because it happens without much conscious thinking on our part.

This does suggest that machines could actually do a pretty good job in analyzing at least part of our behavior and, over time, learn to decipher some of our motives, including our intention when we comment on and subsequently reshare a piece of online content or approach a website for the first time.

Algorithmic trust is of immense interest to anyone who is even remotely involved with the web. It drives some of the results we see displayed on the search engines results pages (SERPs) and it has been of increasing interest since Google search was recoded in 2013 to Hummingbird, to take advantage of relational signals (which is why it's often called semantic search) and try to understand content, queries and end user intent better. The idea behind algorithmic trust is a frighteningly simple one: if we can see exactly who said what to whom and when, for how long and what other people's reaction was to that, we can infer to a high degree of accuracy the importance of that interaction in relation to the item of content it happened over. Do this often enough for a large enough number of people and suddenly you have a handy means of identifying what's true and what isn't. What's important and what may not be.

The "frightening" element of this comes in when you consider the implications of an always-on, always watching, non-human, omniscient observer who then becomes arbiter of facts and truth. This is where Microsoft's of Moritz Y. Becker and Masoud Koleini's *Opacity Analysis in Trust Management Systems*, comes in with its attendant Knowledge Based Trust (KBT) issues that we discussed in Chapter two of this book.

I am going to, for the time being, put aside the scary part of all this for two reasons: First, because we are really not there yet. Knowledge Based Trust is very much a work-in-progress rather than a finished product and at the implementation stage our concerns will be an inevitable part of its execution. Second, because an omniscient, always-on, non-human watcher is not quite as cost-effective from a computational platform point of view as it may sound. The same operational efficiencies that biologically optimize us and strive to save us cognitive computational power apply to a machine. Until we do get a computer with a brain the size of a planet we are left dealing with whatever compromise we can put in place that will give "good enough" results.

So, with these two preconditions in mind, we can look at the calculation of algorithmic trust with a sense of wonder mixed with genuine excitement and we can benefit, directly from our knowledge of it, at least as far as online search is concerned.

Newsfoo used to be an unconference for journalists, technologists and leaders in public policy about the future of news who, trying to keep it real, agreed to forgo the usual paraphernalia of PowerPoint presentations, keynote speakers and pre-planned sessions. The idea behind the invitation-only events was to let spontaneity determine the value of the talks. It's been renamed to Newsgeist and some PowerPoint presentations are allowed, but the invitation-only restriction still holds and those who attend never quite know what to expect.

One of the attendees in the November 14-16 2014 event at the Walter Cronkite School of Journalism and Mass Communication at Arizona State University, was Google's senior director of news and social products, Richard Gingras who in his speech made such mentions as the need to build a "trust framework to enable quality fact-based journalism to rise above the chaos of the internet."

He mentioned that the 1975 landscape of journalism was a little like the medieval village in that the brands were few, their perceived quality high and they enjoyed sufficient trust for our friends, colleagues, family members and classmates to introduce them to us. "Those very same brands today struggle to compete with a cacophonous opinionsphere and a near-malevolent corporate advocacy." But it was in his recap of "The old trust model of trust us because it's us, does not work" that he most accurately summed up the state of play not just of the news industry in the digital era but every business and brand in the world striving to survive in the age of the web.

The problem is that brands that should have found it easy to establish their presence in the new medium didn't because they failed to understand what is different about it. As a result they pressed on with command-and-control methods of marketing, top-down communication and one-way messaging. By doing so they failed to also grasp that the new medium does not just make the process itself look outdated and out of touch but it also renders its mechanism transparent revealing its control freakery for what it is.

When trust is not automatically given to whoever asks for it the loudest and most insistently, reason, says the ones that should receive it are those who have earned it and have been seen to have earned it. Just like in real life. Just like in the small-world medieval village square setting.

It was the father of the web, Sir Tim Berners-Lee who, at the very first World Wide Web Conference in 1994, articulated the semantic web as a vision where the web was no longer just a place consisting of documents for humans to read to one that included data and information for computers to manipulate. The Semantic Web was described back then as a Web that would be capable of actionable information. A place where the logical connection of terms establishes interoperability between systems.

The search that Tim Berners-Lee envisioned back then was one composed of individual Search Agents who could work seamlessly in the background getting you what you wanted as answers rather than web pages that you would need to trawl through yourself. Anyone using Google Voice and getting the answer to the question "Who is the fastest man in the world?" or "Get me pictures of whales" will think that we are just about there. Those who have experienced the predictive magic of Google Now will think that we probably have even exceeded that original vision of search. Both these views would be wrong.

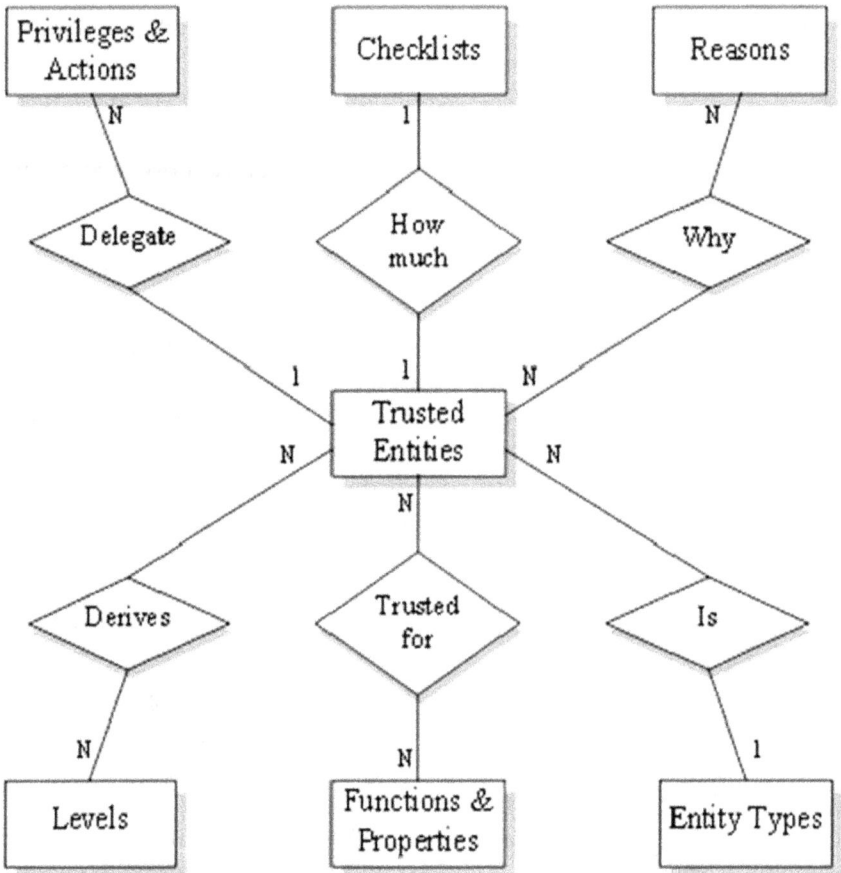

Fig 4.3 – *The web of activity from a trusted entity can allow an algorithm to begin to infer the value that other entities can have in a network. This allows the creation of machine ascribed values for such qualities as authority, expertise and trustworthiness. Semantic search uses machine-ascribed values to determine the relational connections between points of data and better understand their content and context.*

One thing that Tim Berners-Lee visualized in that context was a search intelligent enough not just to retrieve the answers to our questions but also to verify the sources and practically guarantee the results. Veracity the fourth of the four Vs (the other three being Volume, Velocity and Variety) around which Big Data and Semantic Search revolve, is also the trickiest one the get right and, computationally speaking, the most complicated.

Verifying any kind of source is predicated upon search being able to determine, correctly, its history. Provenance, the when, where, who and the conditions under which data originated, has now become a key requirement to a range of applications, search included.

The pay-off here is that the moment semantic search succeeds in its ability to provide verification of the content it serves, automatically, on request, we will reach an entirely new metric for conversions and an entirely new level for competition on Google search.

The understanding is that, in this instance, to show up at all is a win because the website and by inference the business behind that website have been vetted. Its reputation already checked and the verification process itself, transparent. What that is worth to a business can only be left to speculation.

The direction is clear enough to suggest that you should already be taking measures to ensure that there is a hierarchical progression in search that goes from social media visibility to reputation building to search engine content marketing to high visibility in search.

The way trust in results is calculated in the semantic web is predicated upon the ability of search to uncover relational connections and measure the authority of each one. When that happens when there is a high-value definition in a person, an object or a thing, it becomes an Entity and that Entity then needs to be classified.

The process moves information into ever higher levels of abstraction with each Entity of high-trust and verification lending its authority to others when it is relationally connected to them.

Semantic search implies that a reputation algorithm will always be on and it will work roughly the same way that real-life reputation systems work. If, for instance, you wanted to know if you could trust someone to do business with you would, most probably, ask your professional network of contacts.

The chances that someone amongst them will know or have heard about the person you are suggesting to do business with is pretty high. The reason it's high lies in context and relevance. If you are in the business of breeding horses, for example, most of your business network connections will be relevant to your business. Similarly most of the people you will want to do any kind of business with will come from a background that is at least tangential to what you do. There is simply no way someone totally unknown to you and your network of business contacts will pick you out of the blue.

This real world vetting mechanism is based on the Small World theory where connections from any point to any other point are no more than a few degrees of separation away. This also has a direct correlation to the online world because it's based on the idea that you can vet reputation by inferring it from sources. Because semantic reputation networks are essentially social networks they have the Small World properties of connection with the added ability to cache values that have been worked out before and make the calculating process even faster.

In this case trust is treated as a measure of uncertainty in a person or a resource. Specifically, given an ambiguous path where the outcome of a relational transaction such as the purchase of an object can have either a positive or a negative outcome, having trust in a person is defined as a measure of the confidence that the person will take the action that leads to the positive result. Reputation is what you call the measure of that trust.

The point is that in the semantic web trust and reputation are machine-driven and scalable and governed by the Small World theory.

For a business or brand building reputation online the 'plan' begins to become very clear:

- Form as many social connections as possible (i.e. network)
- Leverage your staff to become connection points in the social network marketing of your business
- Create transparency that will allow the establishment of trust and reputation parameters very quickly (make Swift Trust possible)
- Establish a multi-lateral web presence that makes full use of the social media platforms

144

There are a couple of things of deep value to take away from the approach Google has taken on the assessment of Trust, Authority and Reputation. First, the assessment itself, in semantic search is capable of nearly infinite segmentation. It allows for the establishment of trust in specific subjects for instance which means that just as in real life a personal profile that is trusted for recommendations in coffee brands will not enjoy the same level of trust if it switches to let's say cars. The same holds true for websites, companies and brands. Second, trust and reputation are not forever. They hold true as long as there is a freshness in activity. Again, just like real life, the moment a personal profile stops being active or a company or brand stops producing content, their hard-earned trust and reputation begin to evaporate.

When it comes to creating online profiles that will benefit you in semantic search a long-term plan that is sustainable will always work better than a short term one that will produce only temporary results and for that you need continuity, flow, context and relevance.

It sounds like panacea. It's not. At least not quite. In his Online News Association speech for 2015, in Los Angeles, Richard Gingras made the point that "the web has value but does not have values". Again he mentioned trust as the key issue here wondering how it can be used to drive revenue and to grow subscribers.

The web is indeed an open, decentralized distributed computing platform where anonymity still exists in many places. While algorithmic trust is, primarily, search engine driven it is actually people that make it possible. Our online activities, connections, digital identities and digital footprint are signals that mean something. As computers get more powerful and algorithms get smarter it may be feasible to reach the point where the accuracy rate of algorithmic trust will be close to 100%.

At the moment there is still room for improvement and human diligence as well as human action is required to make sure errors are avoided and clarity in social signals is maintained.

Interpersonal Trust

It's Bell Laboratories' Morton Deutsch who gives us the best description of interpersonal trust: "Confidence that [one group] will find what is desired [from another] rather than what is feared." If we start talking about tribes, interagency working groups (like in NYC's Homeland Security) and groups in the workplace interpersonal trust becomes the focal point.

Writing in the *Journal of Applied Psychology*, Olin School of Business, Washington University in St. Louis Professor Kurt Dirks wrote that:

> *"Most of the trust-related research appears to position trust as a variable that has direct (main) effects on work group process and performance. In other words, when the level of trust is increased, a group is expected to experience superior group processes (e.g., higher levels of cooperation) and higher performance; when trust is decreased, a group is expected to experience inferior group processes and lower performance."*

Fig 4.4 – *Interpersonal trust is a key element of commercial organizations and businesses of all types. It is used not just to help teams better harness the capabilities of cooperation and enabling environments and perform at a much higher level than their competitors.*

Dirks is an expert in the steps that need to be taken for trust to be restored once it has been lost of which we shall see a little more about later, but for now it's his work in interpersonal trust between temporary groups that's really of interest.

Such groups occur frequently in the world of business where individuals are brought together to perform a specific task in a tight frame of time. Trust has to be established quickly and its presence or absence has a direct effect on performance.

Dirks' research found that the presence or absence of trust did not seem to have any effect on the quality of the processes that were put in place to get the work down but it did directly affect the group's performance. He was led to conclude that in temporary groups "Trust may be best understood as a construct that influences group performance by channeling group member's energy toward reaching alternative goals."

This should not be so surprising if we remember the definition of trust as a measure of confidence. Teams that have confidence in each other are also happier in their own performance and capable of diverting their full attention to the task they are given to perform.

Sales organizations, retailers and business of all types can benefit directly from a good measure of interpersonal trust.

To make sure it is developed quickly they need:

- Clear boundary setting within the group
- Excellent communication of goals that need to be achieved
- Creating an accepting, non-judgmental culture within the group itself
- Enabling and reinforcing the building of a cohesive group identity
- Clearly quantifying and communicating the value of the work being done

One of the key aspects of interpersonal trust however is that the organizations that succeed in putting it in place benefit strongly from knowledge sharing and the open sharing of expertise, this tends to help develop a much 'smarter' environment where organizations learn faster and share best-practice amongst organization members easiest.

There is an interpersonal trust scale test developed by Dr. J. B. Rotter, Department of Psychology, University of Connecticut, which you can take online: http://goo.gl/PfhOqx.

The final flavor of trust we look at is also the most personal.

Personal Trust

Trust, of course, is always personal. A person who has never trusted and never been trusted will find it difficult to feel trust. He will be unable to extend it to anyone and find it hard to receive any himself. Romulus and Remo, Tarzan and Mowgli may indeed find it next to impossible to accept any trust from humans, their experiences growing up restricted to the primitive and severely circumscribed form of trust that is prevalent amongst members of the animal kingdom.

Personal trust is the hardest of all flavors of trust to examine because it touches upon the red hot raw nerves of our own belief systems. The trust we understand we feel, the very notion of trust we can conceptualize when we are being entirely honest with ourselves, becomes the basis of the trust we are willing to build into the world around us.

Imagine that for a brief moment and suddenly you have grasped the entire difficulty of the issue surrounding trust and why men as respectable as Williamson and North were so eager to completely drop it from their calculations. If you're busy putting in place the building blocks that will make up massive global businesses and even help us better understand how to run the world, the last thing you want to deal with are some ethereal mental tendrils emanating from the deepest recesses of the human mind.

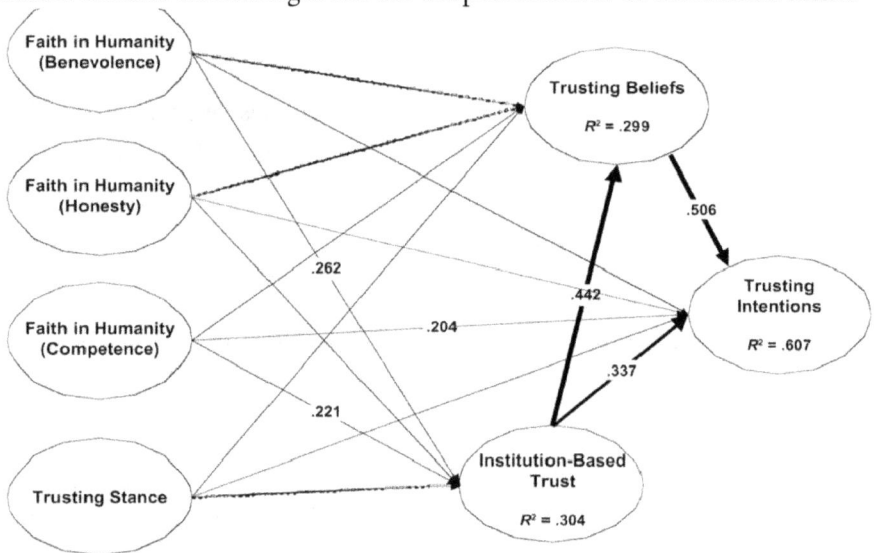

Fig 4.5 – *Personal trust arises out of an intricate web of experiences, beliefs, expectations, intentions and predictions. There are few human actions, as a matter of fact, that do not have at least some foundation in trust.*

Yet, that was the issue with most of the 20th century's operational mode. It treated the individual like he did not matter. It demanded that he put aside his thoughts, bury his inclinations and listen instead to whatever advertising message the particular media channel aimed at him spewed so he can better understand how to maximize the need to consume.

Is it any wonder that we find ourselves, today, in the mess we are in? A world where, VW, the world's largest car manufacturer feels such little respect for the people who buy its products that it is perfectly OK with lying to them, lying to a government, producing cars that damage public health, people's health, and the environment and stealing money from the public purse (by way of tax breaks awarded to it when its car emissions met their target).

It may be unfair to single out VW in this part of the book. There are countless other instances of corporate greed and public manipulation. Bernie Madoff and Enron immediately spring to mind in terms of both damage done and gross abuse of trust.

Because personal trust is so deeply rooted the way it is developed, reinforced, managed and cultivated affects everything else.

As Fig 4.5 shows personal trust is a complex, fragile construct made up of many moving parts. Because it is made up of relational connections we could actually map it and ascribe an ever evolving numeric value to it that would allow us to create an algorithmic trust scale. The obvious stumbling block here is that lacking the ability to accurately read what's hidden deep inside the human brain we can only infer that by observing individual actions, over time.

At the same time we have had the means to know what drives personal trust for a very long time. We understand it because while it is probably different in its exact make up for everybody, in broad strokes the fundamental ingredients are the same for everybody:

- Trust in the intention of others (benevolence)
- Trust in the actions of others (honesty)
- Trust in the capability of others (competence)
- Trust in the constructs of our societies (social trust)

In a study of personal trust in small military teams carried out by

Humansystems Inc., a company that has ties with the military and studies extensively the performance and well-being of people working in complex systems, the researchers found that personal trust in small teams is defined as:

> "*A state involving confident predictions about another's motives with respect to oneself in situations entailing risk*".

And in a further refinement in the same study wrote:

> "*Trust is a psychological state that manifests itself in the behaviors towards others, is based on the expectations made upon behaviors of these others, and on the perceived motives and intentions in situations entailing risk for the relationship with these others.*"

The recurring themes of risk reduction and prediction of a likely, future outcome that have surfaced throughout this book, are also present in this instance. The development of person-based trust is seen as a hierarchical process, in which our views of others become increasingly elaborated as we accumulate information, measure it against our expectations and make what seem rational predictions on how the world works.

Trust then is a social need that allows us to function within society. In his book *The Quiet American* English novelist, Graham Greene, pinpointed trust's liberating value when he wrote: "It is impossible to go through life without trust: that is to be imprisoned in the worst cell of all, oneself."

Liberated by our feeling of trust in others we, as individuals, can take part in social constructs in ways that mirror the focus achieved by groups that are empowered by interpersonal trust. Francis Fukuyama, the economist and political scientist who famously argued in his 1992 book, *The End of History and the Last Man,* that the worldwide spread of liberal democracies and free market capitalism of the West and its lifestyle may signal the end point of humanity's sociocultural evolution and become the final form of human government. Three years later would modify his position by writing about social virtues and the creation of prosperity, where he acknowledged that culture and economics cannot be separated and that trust and the individual's capacity to feel it, are key to the development of the prosperity of nations.

What's good for the economy is also good for business. Helping potential customers develop trust in them and what they do is something companies, businesses and brands are only now beginning to seriously grapple with.

So finally we've come full circle, almost, to crunch point. If personal trust is the kernel round which almost any type of trust is built. If, in the great thicket of trust variants, personal trust is the acorn from which mighty structures can be built it goes to say that it is also key to marketing.

Indeed, Peter Hiscocks, Professor at Cambridge Judge Business School which is part of the University of Cambridge, in England, goes so far as to say that "The ultimate goal of marketing is to generate an intense bond between the consumer and the brand, and the main ingredient of this bond is trust".

Building on his work in a research paper titled "The nature of trust in brands: a psychosocial model" Richard Elliott from the University of Bath and Natalia Yannopoulou from the University of Warwick, both in the UK, identified three steps that lead from personal trust to trust in a brand:

- Familiarity
- Confidence
- Trustworthiness

Familiarity with the brand requires some experience of it (via advertising, word of mouth, internet publicity), Confidence comes with the perception of competence in the brand itself (which is why new brands really need to work hard for people to experience them first) and Trustworthiness refers to the sense of whether the brand is going to live up to its promise of reliability for the price paid.

This is what we can call "The Epson Moment" taken from one of the many interviews of consumers conducted by the researchers of the study:

> Q: *How many printers did you have before buying this one?*
> A: *Well, maybe 7 or 8 printers.*
> Q: *And which brand were they?*
> A: *Well I used to have an Epson perhaps at the beginning but then I switched to Hewlett Packard, they were all Hewlett Packard after that first one.*
> Q: *So what is your perception of the brand?*
> A: *It's reliable, it's good, it's compatible, you can trust it. I think the thing I have is I don't have second thoughts about, I mean I never say maybe this*

will break down, it has never happened at a critical moment so I do trust Hewlett Packard.

Epson used to be a leading name in printers. They were cost-effective, sturdy, reliable. HP managed to steal a march on them by personalizing their company, putting a very human face to the researchers behind the printers in their advertising and company literature and, of course, by living up to the promise they had made.

Were we to use our understanding of this to create a 'brand outreach formula' for a brand trying to connect with its customer base or a company looking to get larger market share or an entrepreneur setting up a business and looking for those core customers he needs, it would look something like this:

- **Commitment** – state clearly what you stand for and honor it

- **Intimacy** – show how you understand your audience needs in detail and think of each individual separately

- **Love/passion** – explain why you do what you do, don't market to some faceless crowd because you happen to make a product you now need to sell

- **Interdependence** – no brand can exist without its customers. An acknowledgment of vulnerability and the mutual dependence of the relationship becomes part of the unwritten contract between a brand and its customers and their shared journey

- **Self-connection** – explain how a customer choosing a brand also expresses or discovers a hidden dimension to themselves. Customers choosing to buy a Rolex when they could buy any other, similarly priced brand are making a statement about themselves as well as the brand

- **Brand partner quality** – be reliable. When consumers give their loyalty to a brand they are invested. They have made a psychological, emotional as well as material commitment. Signs of unreliability feel like intense betrayal to them

- **Trust** – be consistent, defy expectations in a good way, reduce the risk taken by those who have never tried your service or product

Summary

Trust has a strong emotional and psychological component that is not easy to quantify but which drives decisions and motivates actions that have strong, tangible results. While the factors that govern trust in particular settings are setting-specific at times, the overall mechanism of how trust is born and how it develops is very similar.

A 'trust formula' can of course be created but there is none that will be universal and no such formula can be copied. A business that is smart enough to put this into play operates in an environment where it has a close connection between itself and its audience. For a competing business to steal that formula would be courting disaster as there will be significant dissonance between that business' professed beliefs (blindly copied) and actions that have yet to undergo the intricate understanding and alignment that a business has to undergo in order to work in this way.

There are no shortcuts to creating trust. We can algorithmically calculate it in certain contexts and this may well become more and more prevalent as we move forward in our technology and the evolution of the web but how it begins, spreads and becomes established is always part of a very human approach to building relationships.

Paradoxically this is also the case where the relationship in question is between a human and an algorithm or a human and a machine. Trust is experienced in our brains and the way it is developed is irrespective of the nature of the object or person we feel trust for.

In the 21st century trust is the one ingredient that confers a competitive advantage to every type of business. Those that fail to heed this lesson are on a declining course that will only make it more imperative for those who survive to work hard to maintain the consumer trust they have earned.

Five Key Questions to Answer

1. Name five things your business, company or brand do to help establish trust in your target audience
2. Now name five things you do to help ascertain whether that trust is maintained
3. How do you show your customers you really care about them?
4. How do you make your customers feel valued as people, rather than

faceless consumers?

5. Do you have a contingency in case something happens and the trust your customers feel in you is jeopardized?

5

Trust, Loyalty and Reputation

Trust is at its most visible when it makes things happen. Brands rise to the top of consumer preference even when there is no rational price appeal. Nations become more productive. Neighborhoods become safer. Workplaces become happier. People feel, generally, more fulfilled by with where they are and what they do. The elusive species that's called "loyal customer" appears to be everywhere. In this chapter we will look at how all these dots are joined together by the common thread called trust. We shall examine how to make sure it emerges so that all this happens. The affective element of trust is probably the hardest part of it to understand and measure. In this chapter we shall see how this works and why it is so important and how it is part of trust's developmental journey.

This is the secret formula of success of any business or brand: Increase market share, get more loyal customers. It seems simple, rational and straightforward. There is a subtext behind it that gets translated into: do great things that everyone wants to buy or be the kind of company everyone wants to be associated with. Plus, make sure the entire experience of anyone dealing with you is so good that they simply do not want to go anywhere else ever again.

The very fact that so few brands manage to even come close to achieving this is testament enough in the difficulties they face today in making the 'simple' formula I stated above, happen. We've spent most of the book discussing how trust, according to research, is a psychosocial as well as biological response. We saw how biologically we are predisposed to trust because of birth. Trust, we said is a risk-assessment mechanism, a means through which we can gain confidence in decisions we have no right to be confident about ... but. Just like there can be no light without darkness, sound without silence, heat without cold, there really cannot be any sense of trust that exists independently and separately from distrust.

It sounds paradoxical enough to make our heads spin. Does our natural predisposition to trust, evidenced by Cornell University's David Dunning's study on why we trust strangers, make us gullible? Ripe for predation by disowned Nigerian Princes eager to solicit our help to get their hundreds of millions to our country and cut us a generous slice of the action, all for a measly few hundred dollars plus the details of our account?

Does trust, the very same thing that helped us step out of the caves and painfully climb to the very top of the food chain now trip us up by making us gullible? Are we easy to predate upon because we are so willing to trust strangers? What does that say about brands looking to marketers to help them sway our opinion and make purchases that will give them the market share they need?

When you place those questions right next to names like Madoff, Enron, WorldCom, Tyco we naturally begin to question our judgment. Not only that but we also become aware that those we expect to do business with us also begin to question theirs and along with their judgment they begin to suspect that any business they know little about is a suspect one.

It's worth remembering that trust is fragile because, inside the individual who's stepped outside the family environment, it exists in a constant dynamic state of tension with its opposite. Although we are naturally predisposed to trust we are also ready to be convinced to distrust. Our brains are busy calculating what Morton Deutsch described as: "a distrusting choice is avoiding an ambiguous path that has greater possible negative consequences than positive consequences," he was, quite deliberately, stating the exact opposite of his definition for trust and for good reason.

In the era of greater transparency and greater connectivity, where reputations can be checked quickly and information is cheap to obtain there should be no good reason we are duped. Enron and Madoff, to name but two managed to get past the defenses we had in the 20th century and operate as legitimate business because no one was actively looking at them. This is a classic example of the Opacity Analysis in Trust Systems issue that we discussed in Chapter 2 and Chapter 4 of this book.

There were plenty of doubters for both, but in the silo-ed world of the 20th century they did not know where to go and what to do in order to share their suspicions. Left unchallenged two organizations that had no right to exist operated with an attitude of impunity that in hindsight stretches every definition of credulity. There is a behavioral pattern here we will see again. Faced with a challenge they would rather cheat on than work to meet, organizations find shortcuts. When they are not caught, they believe they never will be. They act not just with impunity but with such an air of defiance and self-entitlement that they manage to forestall anyone actively looking at them.

Madoff did just that with his very in-your-face attitude that allowed him to run a Ponzi scheme (named after the Italian-born 1920s swindler who promised 100 per cent profit within 90 days from canny arbitrage with international postal coupons) worth almost $50 billion for half a century, before he was caught.

His approach was exactly like that of Nicholas Levene, the son of an electrician who hardly set the stockbroking world alight, rising from tea boy at Phillips & Drew to the little-known Integrated Asset Management. By 2004, he had amassed a $24.20 million (£16 million) fortune and was living a lifestyle that even his father found "beyond comprehension and understanding".

It grew to include a chauffeur-driven Bentley, $15,000-a-day pheasant shoots, villas in Israel and a $788,000 bar mitzvah party for his son, held in Battersea Park in 2009 and organized by Banana Split – the creatives behind Simon Cowell's 50th birthday bash. Like Madoff, his victims, included some of the sharpest cookies in the business, happy to recommend him to many of their circle.

Louise Brittain, the Deloitte partner who spent three years unwinding Levene's estate since he was declared bankrupt in October 2009, said in a Telegraph article about her work:

"If you look at the personality profile of people like Charles Ponzi, Levene and Madoff they're all much the same – very strong personalities, charismatic, able to emotionally manipulate people. They start small and build trust so they get a ring of people around them happy to recommend them.

"All the returns come through initially, and then what they are very clever at doing is building a bigger network with bigger investments. People join it and start asking questions, but it all seems to stack up – even though the returns on offer are massive and should set the alarm bells ringing. But people like Levene have this ability to make people want to believe them. Then, on the other side, maybe you just have other people's greed."

We've changed. Just like with a virus, each time we fall prey to such massive deceit we put new safeguards in place. While another Madoff or another Enron are unlikely there are still new schemes and scums out there just waiting to trip us up and make us doubt our judgment and misplace our trust. The best inoculation against any and all of them is a sufficiently wide network and a constant, broad flow of information.

It's not that none of the schemes of these conmen were never questioned. They were, but all of them were exceedingly good at presenting an impeccable façade and casting sufficient doubt for the questions to go away. In that act we were complicit. We don't question things too deeply because, as we shall see now, there is a mechanism that should we do, emotionally creates even bigger issues for us than if we do.

We see that there are direct benefits to be had by extending trust in a commercial setting but now we really need to settle the question: If trust is in constant balance with distrust and each time we need to choose between the two why do most of us choose trust over its sibling? Why did so many clever, successful people feel so good about trusting Madoff, Enron, Levene and no one feels equally good when asking difficult questions that should, rightly, be asked?

Social psychologists explain the choice in terms of emotion or rather, emotional energy required. If by extending trust we render the complexity of a picture with many moving parts, simple, because we choose to trust that others which we now depend on, will simply do their job, distrust does not have the same effect.

I may come upon a place on long, dusty road, for example and see a saloon. If I have been walking for a long time, in the blazing sun, I will be thirsty. At that point, in my mind, I need to decide. Do I distrust the saloon? Fear for my life if I enter it and choose to carry on without slaking my thirst. Or do I suppose that the saloon itself has a fairly high cost to set up. That it's function is overseen by the social setting that determines that a saloon at the end of a long, dry an dusty road is an acceptable institution to have and that it is highly likely that once inside all I will have to do is give some money and buy a drink.

While the two choices may seem equally balanced, they're not. If I decide to enter, it means I have decided to trust the saloon and its denizens. I have simplified life because I am now operating under some commonly accepted assumptions that are part of the social contract. More than that I have also accepted that the general place I am in is a benevolent one. That my thirst and fatigue are the only issues I have to contend with. And indeed, once inside the barman asks me what kind of drink I want, tells me how much it is and serves it to me after I have paid.

But should I decide not to enter I am suddenly living in a world of high emotional anxiety. Suddenly the saloon and its territory have been transformed into a hostile zone. I now need to watch my back. My fatigue is a life-threatening issue. I am still thirsty plus I know that if I want to survive in this territory I'd better find some friends, fast and some big guns. I now have huge problems on my hands and no readily available means to solve them.

It is the prospect of higher emotional distress that is associated with open distrust that makes giving trust, where warranted, the more palatable of the two options. It may sound like there is no hope. That in the long term clever conmen and corporations that really want to will still manage to take us for a ride, no matter what. The answer to this is "Yes" and "No". For it to happen we really need to allow the willing suspension of distrust that Georg Simmel said needs to take place, occur. As we saw in Chapter three of this book, without it, trust cannot occur at the Zero Acquaintance stage.

This also suggests that conmen and fraudulent organizations use the exact same mechanism to get past our defenses that legitimate businesses and trustworthy people do. Both want the same thing in the first instance: to convince us that they are worth taking a chance on. But there the similarity ends. Madoff, Levene, Enron, withered under close examination. Their super-power, and they were all exceedingly good at using it, was the lengths they went to, to dissuade people from asking questions, to stop anyone from sharing information about them.

The truth is that for trust to fail we only need to compartmentalize and fragment the world. Make the individual (and even the institution) feel small and powerless. Make whatever entity we had hoped to challenge appear huge, all-powerful, unimpeachable.

Here's what we do know for a fact:

- Even the biggest and most complex institution is made up of people
- People are fallible (and occasionally, greedy)
- No person should be beyond questioning
- No business should be above the law
- Transparency creates vulnerability
- No conmen wants to appear vulnerable
- No institution or organization that cheats welcomes transparency

As it happens, we live in a world that is transparent. We are more and more empowered. Social media and connectivity give us both voice and smarts. We're still learning to use them properly. We should expect to know where anything that can think keeps its brain, before we can trust it, as Rowling so brilliantly suggested.

Trust is a Currency

Let's begin with a fundamental axiom of economics: The ultimate nature of any developed economy is defined by its irreducible qualities or quantities. On a desert planet water becomes a valuable commodity. Its discovery, possession, ownership and use hotly contested actions over which complex legal, political, philosophical and social implications will arise.

In our digital, ever developing, ever more and more connected world there are just two fundamental qualities that eventually give value to anything:

Attention and Trust. They are both intimately linked. With only 24 hours to the day and more and more voices vying for our attention, where we decide to give it is a question of trust. Having one's attention without being able to gain their trust is self-defeating. You cannot gain anyone's trust without having their attention. You cannot have their attention if you're not an authority.

This is not the Authority of biblical definition but you must be an authority in what you do, the same way that Google, for instance is regarded as being an authority in search (though we might make a convincing case for them being the Authority in that area), just like Apple is considered to be an authority in design or Amazon an authority in local and international online shopping.

Here's how you get to be that authority:

* Identity
* Conversations
* Sharing
* Presence
* Relationships
* Reputation
* Groups/communities

If you do not have a say, presence, brand awareness or brand recognition in these seven areas, each of which also constitutes a step in your online marketing activity then you are not an authority, the attention you get will be, at best, incidental and ephemeral and your ability to command the trust of those you deal with will also reflect those qualities.

It was these steps which allowed John Lewis in the UK to rise to the #1 position in shopper's trust and preferences when Amazon, while doing nothing wrong, became tainted with its policy of legal tax avoidance. This is how fragile trust is. By placing its payment-taking subsidiary in the low tax jurisdiction of Luxembourg, Amazon was able to get away with paying just over $15 million to the public purse, in the UK, through corporation tax in a decade. In the meantime its British sales over the previous four years alone were over $35 billion.

The story broke in 2014 and a May article carried in *The Guardian* urged shoppers to boycott Amazon. Considering that a similar story and a similar strategy had made Starbucks develop a social conscience and decide to not use the tax avoidance opportunities legally available to it and pay, instead, UK corporation tax, it was evident that history was going to repeat itself.

A year later, almost to the day, Amazon announced that UK sales were being processed in the UK which made the company liable for paying full UK taxes.

The Amazon case (and Starbucks, before it) was a case of broken social trust. "Social trust is a belief in the honesty, integrity and reliability of others – a 'faith in people'" starts a 2007 Pew Research Center survey which concludes that "…people who feel vulnerable or disadvantaged, for whatever reason, tend to find it riskier to trust because they're less well-fortified to deal with the consequences of misplaced trust."

Trust is a projection of hope that take into account the other party's intent. In a nightclub, for example, I may hope to get to my table from the bar, across the dance floor with my martini glass, held aloft, unspilled. In my calculation I take into account the fact that none of the other people around me will intentionally bump into me, as I negotiate my way through them. The moment intention is factored in and I discover that they are all there to make sure that my glass of martini never gets to my table, my task becomes hopeless. My cause is lost.

Amazon (and Starbucks) intentionally engaged in legal maneuvers that withheld money from the public purse of the countries their operations were thriving from. Their actions were hurting local businesses which did not have the same advantage and damaging the county's local economy by creating unemployment, generating deflationary measures and creating conditions where fair competition could not, generally, thrive in.

The sense of public outrage caused by this resulted in their suffering a direct loss in profits. This is the effect of what researchers Cristiano Castelfranchi and Rino Falcone, writing a paper on social trust for the National Research Council - Institute of Psychology, called "Internal Attribution" theory. They were looking at the components of social trust both locally and globally which is why the Amazon and the Starbucks cases fit in so beautifully.

Social trust is a cognitive process made up of:

- Internal attributions (derived from our calculation of the probability of willingness, persistence, engagement, competence)
- and External attributions (derived from our calculation of the probability of having the appropriate conditions, opportunities and resources)

Amazon and Starbucks, like any large business were persistent, engaging and certainly competent to deliver on what they promised. They also had the necessary knowledge and awareness to act for the public good, to not willfully hurt local businesses and the local economy, to –in other words, act responsibly in a way that allowed us to sense they were trustworthy as an institution.

That was the component they reneged on, in the equation and both paid a hefty, customer-imposed penalty on.

Their tale shows us something: trust works because we all believe in it. Companies that act irresponsibly, companies that behave like it does not really matter as long as they deliver on what they promise, which should be enough, are companies we are increasingly reluctant to deal with.

Amazon and Starbucks did nothing illegal, though their actions were construed as being immoral. Now juxtapose this against the seriousness of the VW case:

- VW knowingly used its technical expertise to install "device defeat" software in 11 million cars, worldwide that were being sold as being "environmentally friendly".
- The alleged (and now shown to be wrong) technical specifications of its vehicles allowed the company to claim Federal Tax Breaks in the US that had been established under the Energy Policy Act of 2005.
- Their NOx emissions (up to 40 times higher than the EPA approved levels) knowingly harmed public health in cities and towns.
- In the description of their environmentally friendly vehicles they made, unwitting, accomplishes to environmental damage and public health, of people who are genuinely concerned about these things.
- They became the world's largest car maker, ahead of Toyota, based on a lie.

There are several cases of operational (i.e. faith in the product), interpersonal (faith in the company) and social (faith in the company's intentions and morality) trust broken there and then. And this before we get to any revelations of high-level conspiracy to commit fraud that may come out.

Trust will not make you money if your product is not good, if your business model is outmoded or if there is no market for what you're selling. But if you do have something everybody wants, if your business is capable of delivering and if you are constantly evolving the way you operate, trust will make it possible for you to succeed.

Trust is what monetizes the attention economy.

Trust is what turns occasional customers into loyal ones who are passionately engaged with the businesses they deal with.

John Lewis, in the UK, overtook Amazon, and recorded a 6% rise in profits, as a result, because it remained true to its principles, showed it cared and became, in the customers' minds, more personal and personalized than at any other time before. This, alone, did not materially affect any purchasing decisions. It is highly unlikely that upon hearing that John Lewis had claimed the moral high ground in the way they operated, there were customers who woke up one day with the overriding thought to go and shop there.

Affective responses to brand impact however work deep. Having the attention of its public John Lewis was able to better capitalize on it when their purchasing journey started. Being perceived as a moral choice, as well as a clever one, to shop at one of its stores or its website made customers feel good about themselves and their choices. This is Identification Based Trust (IBT) which in trust's developmental journey is the most desirable stage for a business to reach. At that point, the business and its customers have a near-perfect alignment of values and goals. The business needs only to focus on how to translate that alignment into profit for itself and real value for its customers.

Playing the Loyalty Card

Type into Google search "Why Are Customers Loyal?" and you will get page after page with results like "10 tips to keep customer loyalty", "Build customer loyalty with these 18 proven strategies" – you get the drift. If customer loyalty was truly understood supermarkets wouldn't have brought out point-based "Loyalty Cards" which in reality are bribery cards where they pay us in points for things we will purchase already, hoping we will then spend just a little more than we plan so we can get the money voucher that we can spend only with them.

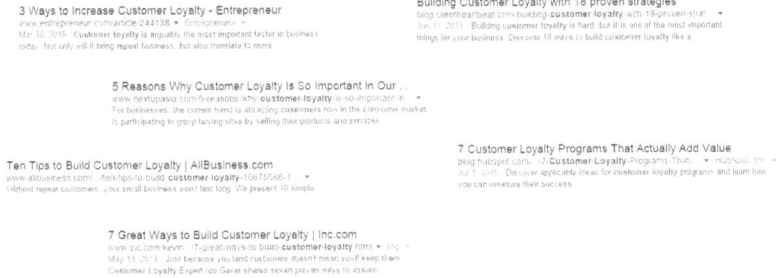

Fig 5.1 – *We look at customer loyalty like it's a secret recipe that we somehow need to crack, forgetting the fact that what keeps a customer loyal is the same thing that keeps a business honest: great quality, great service at a price that makes sense and a passion for maintaining all this.*

Any first-year primary school kid with a bagful of sweets and in need of making some friends will tell you that loyalty cannot be bought and it really cannot be strategized for in the hard sense of the word. Which, of course, begs the question why do consultants, marketers, business strategists and some of the world's largest brands think that loyalty can be bought if only they find the magic formula of steps that captures their audience's love?

A business, a brand or a company that has loyal customers is:

- Less vulnerable to competitive marketing actions
- Able to reduce marketing costs
- Able to enjoy higher rates of return on investment (ROI)
- Going to get a greater market share
- Better able to enjoy cooperation with intermediaries
- Going to get more favorable word of mouth publicity
- Capable of taking full advantage of greater extension opportunities

All of this is powered by a deep sense of trust which, at consumer level, is often referred to as brand trust which has an additional monetary layer of value when we factor in brand equity. Coca-Cola, which topped Interbrand's, a corporate identity and brand consulting company, list since it started compiling it in 2000; is valued at $79.2 billion.

In 2013, it lost the No #1 slot to Apple who also overtook it in brand equity with an estimated price tag of $98.3 billion. Underscoring the subtle combination of consumer loyalty and trust and its impact on the bottom line Interbrand's 2013 report begins:

"Every so often, a company changes our lives, not just with its products, but with its ethos. This is why, following Coca-Cola's 13-year run at the top of Best Global Brands, Interbrand has a new No. 1 — Apple."

The reason most marketers will shy away from the trust component when considering how to create loyalty in their customers while, like supermarkets, they will focus on the cognitive aspects of the equation (most of which give a reply to the question "what's in it for me?") is the same one that made Oliver Williamson and most 20th century businesses shy away from it: metrics.

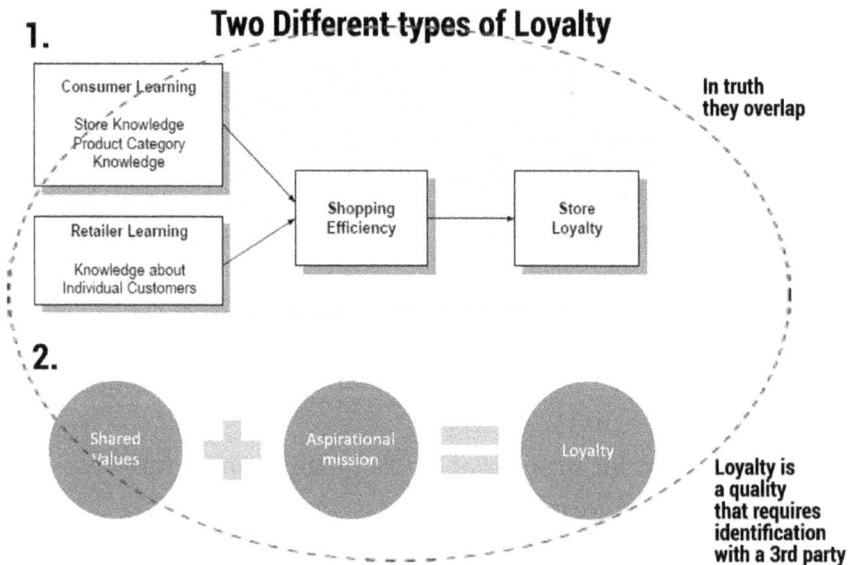

Fig 5.2 – *There is a strong overlap between the cognitive and affective elements that go into creating trust in a business, a company or a brand.*

If you're looking at 'loyalty' metrics that go by the name of "number of card holders" or "number of signed up accounts" or (even worse) "number of repeat customers" you're more than likely are thinking in terms of 20th century business models and are failing to take into account brand trust. This, almost certainly, suggest that you're also failing to take into account the value proposition and how it is reflected in your customers' aspirations and your own working values and ethos and how they align with those of your audience.

Customer loyalty has two parts which are roughly equal, always in flux and re-calculated, the same way they would be in any real relationship. One part is cognitive (and rests on calculative trust which looks at potential risk and potential rewards as part of the relationship) and the other part is affective (which has a strong emotional component and attaches emotional and aspirational values to the connection between a person and a brand).

The cognitive part is as seductive as a Jonathan Mizel squeeze page. Mizel is credited with having invented the long form sales-pitch that runs what is supposed to be the "yes?", "no?" "why?" conversation that would take place between a salesperson and a prospect had they met face-to-face. On the web this translates into a seemingly endless sales page that lists benefits, tries to assuage doubts, asks that irksome "still not convinced?" question, includes jubilant video, picture or signed letter testimonials from people no one's ever heard of but who unreservedly endorse the product, it includes highlighted text and capitalized points in blue or red (playing on our color psychology) and always ends with a 'limited' time offer for a massive discount, supposedly adding to the psychological pressure felt by the prospect, overcoming any natural resistance barriers and leading to an online sale. And, just to completely overcome any possible risk-aversion response, there is always a 100% satisfaction guaranteed, money back pledge.

As you probably guessed I've never been a big fan of such pages. Mizel used to sell insurance (and hated it) and he transferred a lot of what he learnt plying his trade to the web. It works if you're desperate and don't have a choice and desperately need to be convinced that this will work for you and become your way out of whatever dead-end you find yourself in. That is the real target audience of these squeeze pages.

The rest of us hate them, but marketers love them. The layout, flow logic and structure allows them to visualize a real dialogue with a cornered person in a face-to-face situation and tinker with the on-page psychological triggers hopping to wear any resistance the online visitor may have, down.

What Makes This Simple Marketing Funnel Formula So Consistently Effective At Giving Even The Most Novice Online Marketers Their First $100,000 Sales Machine In Under 30 Days?

Fig 5.3 – *If you're a millennial and have not had any experience of the pushy door-to-door salesman technique, relax. Squeeze pages like this are still around the web.*

That is exactly the approach taken by those who use only the cognitive element of loyalty, itemizing every single benefit that explains why their brand is the only rational choice and then throwing a massive reward bonus point scheme if you use your loyalty card, as a clincher.

What the approach forgets is that consumers are not faceless money bots whose buttons need to be pressed so they can drop their money in a business. They are living, breathing, thinking, judging and now, freely communicating, loud, visible human beings.

They want to feel that:

- They matter
- They are listened to
- They are worth communicating with
- They have aspirations that are in tune with yours
- Your ethos and theirs is in perfect sync

If you cannot show all of that, you are not really considering your target audience. You shouldn't really have any expectation of consideration back from them.

Truth is that whether you're a one-person outfit or a 300K-staff corporation, whether you're working online or offline or in any mix of the two, the only way you will gain trust in what you do and be able to convert that into brand equity is if you can show, consistently and over time that you treat your customers with the same care and respect that you would like to be treated yourself.

John Lewis, in the UK, learnt that a long time ago and has never lost sight of the fact. In the 21st century most businesses are having to either learn it anew or see their profitability fade away.

In the early days of social media many large brands took this as a signal that "they should be our friends". The perception was not helped much by the focus on Facebook marketing and its Like button (for brand pages) which was very much like befriending.

Media coverage of this is a tale of woe: "We want to be your friend" cries out an article on brands written in *The Economist* where it says:

> *"Consumers are bombarded with brands wherever they look—the average Westerner sees a logo (sometimes the same one repeatedly) perhaps 3,000 times each day—and thus are becoming jaded. They are also increasingly familiar with the tricks of the marketing trade and determined to cut through the clutter to get a bargain. Scepticism and sophistication are especially pronounced among those born since the early 1980s."*

The subheading to the article is that: Brands are finding it hard to adapt to an age of scepticism.

"Brands aren't your friends, they're the idiots at the social media party" says another headline in the tech blog *The Next Web*. Where the writer points out that:

> *"Of course brands screw up a lot on social media. It's because, despite their rictus grins, the plastic masks of friendship they wear are just hiding the fleshy, flawed faces of underpaid social media people, who are often trying to be the fun voice of several soulless logos at once."*

"Brands: Consumers Don't Want to Be Your BFF in Social (They Want Help)" screamed an *Advertising Age* lead article with the subheading *Enough with 'Chatvertising' -- Users Want Service, Not Friendship. Advertising Age* is read by industry people so the penny may be about to drop, if it hasn't already.

Loyalty is, indeed based on an affective response as well as a cognitive one, but the affective response comes from meeting people's direct needs when they use a service or product and becoming an essential part of their lives.

Think how hard it would be to do any kind of research, find anything to buy, discover new facts or even write this book, if Google search suddenly vanished. Our affective response there would be pretty darned strong, which means that there is one in place already, underpinning the more cognitive approach that says that Google search is more responsive, accurate and reliable than any other kind of search engine available on the market today.

Indeed, researchers Kurt Matzler, Sonja Grabner-Kräuter, Sonja Bidmon writing a paper published in *Innovative Marketing* listed the following moderators in the complex relationship between brand trust, brand loyalty and the perception of value:

- Gender and age
- Involvement
- Price consciousness
- Brand consciousness

None of this is new, any more than anything that has to do with trust is new. The horseshoe maker in the medieval village square knew that his clientele had a core demographic, that the involvement of any of them with his product and his business depended upon the level of personal relevance his horseshoes had for them, all of them were conscious about his prices and the relationship he developed with them was the only thing that stopped them from buying from his competitor in the neighboring village.

In terms of how we do business our technology may be more advanced but our methods aren't. If anything many a business or a brand could do better by picking up tips from the medieval market place.

Summary

Brand loyalty and brand reputation have a direct impact on a company's or brand's bottom line. The perception of what a brand is, what it stands for and the way it operates affects consumer behavior and can make a significant difference in market share and sales. Brands that forget to humanize themselves and then forget that customers are individuals with their own goals and aspirations, soon find themselves operating at a disconnect with their target audience. Relationship building is an unavoidable part of brand building and doing business, today.

Five Key Questions to Answer

1. How does your business or brand measure customer loyalty?
2. What metrics do you use to measure customer satisfaction?
3. How do you communicate with your customers?
4. How do you think the way you communicate with your customers makes them feel?
5. Do you think there is a gap in your perception of how trusted your brand or business is and how your customers feel about it?

6

Losing and Regaining Trust

Trust is a paradox because it is both fragile and robust at once. It is so highly dependent upon the quality of the relationships a business or brand establishes with its customers that each case where a trust issue occurs is unique. A lot depends on the brand's reputation, the seriousness of the transgression, the conditions around it and its handling. Just like any kind of relationship a case of broken trust has the potential to completely derail a brand and destroy its value or it can become an opportunity that will help it get closer to its customers. In this chapter we shall examine cases that fall into each category, look at the very recent, still breaking VW scandal and see exactly what is the process of rebuilding trust and how it can be applied.

Along with some great music and bad hairstyles, the 1980s gave to the world two corporate disaster scenarios that had they been deliberately designed they could not have been more opposite in handling and outcome. Both are intricate enough to warrant a book in themselves. For our purposes however the broad outline will suffice.

The first is the Union Carbide Bhopal disaster in India, when on the night of 2–3 December 1984, a series of systemic, staff and design problems resulted in one of the world's worst industrial disasters, adversely affecting over 500,000 people. Union Carbide tried to handle this in a very traditional way by immediately denying culpability which it passed onto its Indian subsidiary and, much later, claimed sabotage.

Through mediation with the Indian government the Indian Supreme Court the company eventually admitted some moral responsibility and paid $470 million, a relatively small amount based on significant underestimations of the long-term health consequences of exposure and the number of people exposed. The constant drain on resources, the effect of the incident on stocks share price and the subsequent low morale at the company adversely affected the fortunes of a corporation that, until the disaster happened, had straddled the world. The name Union Carbide became synonymous with corporate greed in some circles. Some of the most profitable assets of the company were dismantled and sold off. Union Carbide abandoned its Indian factory without cleaning it up. The toxic chemicals left behind contaminated the land and poisoned the underground water surrounding communities depended on.

To this day there are petitions being put together and sent to the White House to pressure the company to clean up Bhopal, much as BP was forced to clean up the Gulf. The name Union Carbide continues to stand as a symbol of corporate negligence and indifference. Dow Chemicals, the company that bought what was left of Union Carbide has itself suffered reputationally. Its stocks and shares as well as overall performance tainted by its acquisition.

The second case study to come out of that era actually predated the Bhopal disaster by a couple of years and it involved Johnson & Johnson. This time it was a case of product tampering when Tylenol, the nation's favorite pain killer was tampered with. Tylenol Extra-Strength capsules were replaced with cyanide-laced capsules, the packages were then resealed, and deposited on the shelves of at least a half-dozen or so pharmacies, and food stores in the Chicago area. Seven people died a horrible death as a result and the media went into overdrive.

Before the crisis, Tylenol was the most successful over-the-counter product in the United States with over one hundred million users. It was responsible for 19% of Johnson & Johnson's corporate profits during the first 3 quarters of 1982. It accounted for 13% of Johnson & Johnson's year-to-year sales growth and 33% of the company's year-to-year profit growth. Tylenol was the absolute leader in the painkiller field accounting for a 37% market share, outselling the next four leading painkillers combined, including Anacin, Bayer, Bufferin, and Excedrin. Had Tylenol been a corporate entity unto itself, profits would have placed it in the top half of the Fortune 500.

The incident, which had nothing to do with how the company manufactured and sold its product had the potential to destroy all of that and Johnson & Johnson's reputation with it. What happened next has become a textbook case on how to handle a reputation crisis. The Johnson & Johnson management team led by James Burke, reacted to the negative media coverage by forming a seven-member strategy team. The team's strategy guidance from Burke was first, "How do we protect the people?".

Johnson & Johnson went into the offensive, recalling every single one of its Tylenol products and communicating its actions to the media. It made history by creating the first tamper-proof medicine bottles and throughout the crisis it went into extraordinary lengths to create transparency in all its actions, lead the conversation to focus on the facts of the case and its efforts to restore safety in the public domain.

Within a year of the crisis Tylenol and Johnson & Johnson had returned to pre-crisis level profits and the amount of trust the company enjoyed from the public exceeded any of its competitors who were only then, following in its wake, introducing tamper-proof medicine bottles of their own.

"Trust, like the soul, never returns once it is gone" says Publilius Syrus in his collected moral sayings. Publilius was Roman slave brought over from Syria to Rome sometime between 85 BC and 43 BC. He was quick-thinking and witty and won his freedom from his master who also educated him. He spent the rest of his life in Rome, making a living out of his aphorisms and mime theatre, which he performed himself.

If we are to be guided by his words alone two things will happen: first, we will have to agree that there is no hope for VW anymore and this section in the chapter will be a very short one and second, I will have made the mistake of forgetting that trust is contextual and rooted in culture. As a largely psychosocial construct it mutates over time as our social constructs evolve.

The Johnson & Johnson, Tylenol case argues that trust can be regained, so luckily for VW (and me) while trust is today just as important as it was in Roman times, we understand a lot more about how it works to know that when it is broken there can be remedies that can be applied to help repair it. The downside to this is that repairing trust in a relationship where it has been broken is not easy and unless the actions taken to address the repair are themselves thorough and credible, they will not be enough.

But let's begin with some easy steps first. Any case of broken trust is likely to include a number of factors. Some of these will affect perceived competence, others perceived integrity and others still social culpability. The actions taken to regain lost trust hinge on three primary aims (all of which incidentally were achieved in the Tylenol case):

- Repair trustworthiness that has been damaged
- Restore positive exchange in the transactional process between two parties
- Reduce negative affect that has been created as a result of the betrayal of trust

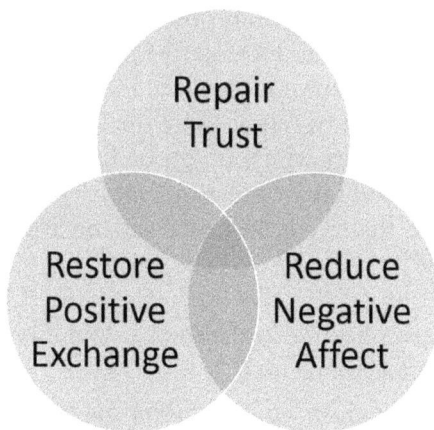

Fig. 6.1 – *Regaining trust once it has been lost is the Venn Diagram between the actions taken to address the loss of trust, the re-establishment of value in the relational exchange between two parties and the reduction of adverse emotions in the relationship.*

It is a common mistake made amongst brands and marketers to think that the damage done to a brand suffering from a sudden loss of trust is something momentary that can be calculated in immediate balance sheet numbers, which can then be fixed quickly.

Two case studies show just how wrong this short-term approach is and the complexities involved in finding a fix. First let's consider Starbucks in the UK. As the economic recession hit its second year in the UK the BBC run a story on Starbucks showing that a Reuters Investigation had uncovered that the US coffee giant had reportedly paid just $13.04 million (£8.6m) in corporation tax in the UK over 14 years.

The tax avoidance scheme used by Starbucks may have been complicated and a little disingenuous, it was not however illegal. A Starbucks spokesperson at the time was quoted saying "We do this in a way that is consistent with the values that have guided us since we were founded more than 40 years ago: balancing our need to operate a profitable business with a social conscience."

The social outcry however was such that it brought together mass media channels and social media ones and soon a boycott of its coffee was organized. In a lesson that was to be learnt by Amazon a couple of years later, Starbucks relented and changed its profit reporting practices so that it paid full corporation tax in the UK.

The fix, here, obviously was an obvious one. Starbucks needed to start paying its taxes just like any other local coffee place it was competing with. A short-term approach could have fudged the issue, calculating, for example that a refusal to do anything not required by the law would result perhaps in a 3% - 4% loss of customers which might be fine and certainly less than what paying full corporation tax would cost. But it's really not that simple. A number of intangibles that are linked by trust and are affected by its breach, come into play:

- Starbucks advertises heavily in the media. Would its adverts suddenly have a negative affective result?
- Would a sense of illegitimacy begin to erode its market share?
- Would people still want to work for a company tainted with public ill will?

These are factors that create a steady bleed effect on brand equity. They accumulate until the pressure of a downward spiral becomes inexorable and the company finds it very difficult to recover. Luckily for Starbucks, it responded quickly with a full, transparent fix and helped restore its tarnished image.

In even deeper hot water with a more complex fix required is VW. As we saw in the earlier part of this chapter, in the section where we examined the value of trust as currency in the attention economy the car maker is in breach of a number of different types of trust and has also acted illegally. Getting out of its predicament is not going to be easy, not least because the actors in this drama are not just a brand and its customers as we had in the cases of Amazon and Starbucks, but also local and Federal governments whose laws the company knowing and willfully, breached.

Bearing in mind that a loss of trust may be as subtle as the loss of confidence in the morality and integrity of a company that UK consumers experienced with Amazon and Starbucks or as complicated as the gross betrayal of confidence in the product and a loss of trust in the company's competence to deliver it, which we have with VW the actions that lead to recovery, themselves have many working parts and need to take full account of the customer and all injured parties.

As a matter of fact, the one, overriding difference between a company trying to repair lost trust to its brand today and what used to happen in the past is found in the fact that in the 21st century its success or failure no longer depends upon its own actions alone. There are good reasons for that and in listing them all we also describe the differences of the world we live in today as opposed to what used to happen on the other side of the millennium.

When a brand's logo, values, ethos and reputation were a carefully crafted, canned message that only required a large enough advertising budget to 'get across' brands could confidently control what happened to them, the perception of what they did and what they were worth and how trustworthy they appeared.

When things did go wrong it was only a question of scale which then determined how long the problem would retain the attention of the Press (and therefore the public) which would also define the extent and cost of the PR response. Clearly that 'gentlemanly' way of dealing with brand scandals has gone.

In the internet age everything is front page, all the time. The conversation around an issue happens much faster and, usually, outside the 'sanctioned' mass media channels where a brand's PR staff may have some reach and influence and unless the answers are credible and the effort to make amends and truly rebuild trust bridges that have been destroyed is credible the problem is not going to go away. A brand's fate today is held, quite literally in the hands of its audience: its fans, its customers and its detractors who also need to be taken into account.

Three 'Little' Things

The set of options available when trust has been broken fall into just three categories:

- Apology
- Denial
- Promise

When analyzed into its component parts restoring trust is a process that is even more complicated than the one that creates it in the first place. The reason for this lies in the insubstantial and largely subjective form that trust takes in the first instance.

Because trust is largely a belief system, a personal framework that allows confidence to enter the mechanism of predicted outcomes in situations where the rational level of analysis is either low or absent, repairing it is more than a case of making up for what has been damaged or is missing.

When trust is broken what happens is that the conditions arise for two parties that were previously connected by a common bond of trust, to suddenly be separated by conflicting belief systems. By choosing one of the three options available to it, a company that suffers from a trust issue also chooses the framework within which the conflict resolution of differing ideas and perceptions can now take place.

Within that it is worth examining the three options available, seeing the different elements that are called into play every time a decisions is made to address a crisis of trust with one of the options available and also identifying corporate behavior from the examples we've already seen:

- **Apology** – The trust-violator admits culpability. He exhibits genuine remorse and says he is willing to take responsibility and do whatever it takes to regain trust. An apology can positively affect the evaluation of motivation and intent and it addresses the question whether the violation of trust will continue. Research on trust repair includes two aspects: trust belief and trust behavior. In order for trust to be regained both trust belief and trust behavior need to be shown to have changed.

- **Denial** – The trust-violator refuses to assume responsibility for whatever has happened. He cites other reasons as the primary cause. Denial is divided into types - direct denial and indirect denial. Direct denial is when the trust-violator claims that what is being claimed against him is not true. Indirect denial is when the trust-violator points to a "scapegoat" and suggests all responsibility lies with the scapegoat, rather than him. Those who go down this path, exhibit no sense of guilt or remorse.

- **Promise** – In this scenario the trust-violator acknowledges the relationship between him and his audience and makes specific promises to improve it. These may involve paying reparations, making tangible changes to his process or submitting to a judicial inquiry as part of the trust-rebuilding process.

Kurt Dirks, whose research on trust we encountered in Chapter four of this book, says:

> "...the repair of trust is the result of cognitive and interpersonal processes through which people resolve differences in their interpersonal beliefs"

In a complex paper titled "The Repair of Trust: A Dynamic Bi-Lateral Perspective and Multi-Level Conceptualization" published in the *Academy of Management Review* he explains that when trust is broken, what is really at work is a breach of a psychological contract.

For instance, a baker who refuses to bake bread one day, and presents his customers with empty shelves when they come to make a purchase may think he could easily fix the problem by simply baking bread later, or baking bread again the next day but this is not actually going to work. Some customers will feel a certain degree of uncertainty over the fact that bread was not presented when promised. Simply fixing it is not sufficient to overcome the uncertainty introduced by his actions or the feeling of annoyance and even betrayal experienced by his customers.

Instead he will have to launch into a full explanation of why bread was not baked that day and explain why this will now never happen again. Even then, he will be on probation until, with time, his customers are satisfied that he has indeed addressed the issue.

The example of the baker is an innocuous one. Still consider that perhaps a percentage of his customers, having experienced no bread for sale one day, look to make other arrangements and some never come back. In order to win those back the baker now needs to launch a full-out information offensive, complete with special offers and perhaps even a voucher offering a substantial discount on a one-off purchase to those who come back.

It already got complicated and no loaves of bread were hurt, no customers died of hunger and no riots happened outside the bakery. Suppose one (or all three) of these things had happened in addition to the no-bread-for-sale day, would that baker have a future again? Would the bakery? What if the bakery publicly replaced the baker? Alleged sabotage by a baker who had simply had enough of a life behind the scenes, baking bread?

Dirks says that trust repair without full engagement of the audience is next to impossible and cites the approach as a classic mistake made in pre-21st century research. The first thing VW did as its emissions scandal broke out was to get rid of its CEO under whose watch the scandal took place, appoint head of Porsche division, Matthias Müller, as new CEO and blame a 'small group' of staff for the scandal.

Speaking in *The Guardian* on the issue Bernd Osterloh, chairman of Volkswagen's work council and a member of the executive committee, said: "A small group has done damage to our company. We need a climate where mistakes are not hidden."

In the same article and in tacit acknowledgment of the challenge facing him Müller said:

> "My most urgent task is to win back trust for the Volkswagen Group – by leaving no stone unturned and with maximum transparency, as well as drawing the right conclusions from the current situation,"

Trust is formed of both trusting beliefs and an understanding of trusting motivations and intentions. Trust-violations affect both of these and getting them back will take a concerted, meticulous approach that addresses every instance of doubt that may arise in the mind of those who have been affected by the violation of trust.

Even worse, trust violations result in loss of trust in those who are not affected directly by the incident. Using the VW case again, at the time of this book going to press, the social media platforms were abuzz by speculation as to how deep the issue was at VW and how widespread it might be in the car manufacturing industry as a whole.

Many of those who took part in long, heated debates did not drive VWs and may have never been a VW customer. To repair its reputation VW now needs to also address their issues, directly, at a conceptual rather than material level.

Adding to the long list of paradoxes associated with trust is the fact that while a brand may work really hard to build trust with its audience and benefit directly from that in terms of sales, loyalty and increased market share, behavior that leads to a loss of trust taints not just the brand in question that is affected directly, but also, indirectly every brand like it, active in its industry.

The popular saying "it takes just one bad apple to spoil the barrel" also applies here.

Can 'Enemies' Become Friends?

Hidden behind the attempts to regain trust lost, lies the question whether it is at all possible to reverse a situation that has become adversarial to the point that it can now become workable again. Once loyal customers, feeling betrayed, can turn into bitter enemies. Once great partners can feel that they have been badly let down. An entire ecosphere that was a brand's market share can feel so disenfranchised that to actively make the decision to move away.

In recent memory such a Waterloo moment for a global brand was supplied by Research in Motion (RIM) the owners of Blackberry. At their peak, in 2007, the company was selling 15 million Blackberries a quarter, it was softly killing Apple and it was the world's most valuable tech company, synonymous with the terms "aspirational", "super-cool" "smartphone". The phone was the must-have device for businessmen, the super-cool accessory of choice of Hollywood stars and the phone that was seen in the hands of Barrack Obama, Hilary Clinton and global heavyweights in almost any scene that needed to show how hip and 'with it' and tech-savvy the users were.

Four years later, in 2011, while struggling to meet changing consumer demands the company was still doing great with more than 70 million global subscribers as of Sept. 15 that year, a whopping 40% growth over the previous year. It was not a good moment to alienate them.

In October 2011 RIM suffered the worst outage in its history in both length and breadth. A tech company suffering a technical glitch should not have been news. It became a global story because of the poor handling of the crisis. With customers globally depending on its servers RIM kept Canadian office hours and that included its social media teams. The BlackBerry service outage started in Europe, the Middle East and Africa but it soon spread to South America and Canada. By the time the social media team had fired its Twitter account and happily chirped "Hello Blackberry users. How may we help you?" Twitter in the UK was experiencing near meltdown with irate business owners who had been effectively locked out of their business emails.

Handled sensitively RIM might have ridden this out. The year was 2011, social media was a thing. News and reactions moved quickly, consumer emotions were highly visible. RIM's announcement that it would be holding a PR announcement about its outage at midday UK time did not go down particularly well. By the time it was resolved, a few days later the crisis had cost the company a huge loss of trust. It had tainted a brand that was fighting with Apple's iPhone for consumers' affection and the then burgeoning Android phone, with a sense that it was untrustworthy and, suddenly, unnecessarily expensive.

The share price plunged from an all-time high of $149.90 to just $11.91 on May 2012 speaks volumes about consumer sentiment for the once-loved (and now renamed to simply "Blackberry") tech company.

Still, the question remains, is it possible to mend bridges? The answer lies in research taken directly from the United States' impressive list of one-time enemies, now turning strategic trading partners and yes, even close friends. Britain (its once colonial master) is an obvious case here but that may be an aberration driven, to some extent, by a sense of shared culture and language and the argument that the alignment of shared values was already in place. So, let's add to it: Japan, Vietnam, China, and Germany.

Contact Theory proponents have been quick to point out the humanizing influence of bringing people in conflict, together, so that they can overcome their differences and find a workable, cooperative solution that benefits both sides. The process hinges on a number of carefully orchestrated steps designed to reduce risk and gradually increase the missing trust factor:

- **Remove conflict**: It is necessary to agree that continued conflict achieves little and that a workable solution requires its removal.
- **Mutual interdependence**: Where one party can safely pull out, then this position of power can destroy common understanding. There has to be a gradual alignment of positions and values to tie both parties into a more symmetrical relationship.
- **Equal status:** If one party has advantages that the other does not, then this again unbalances power. While there may well be status differences in terms of say, a company and its customers, there has to be a perception of equal power and respect.
- **Positive contact:** The context for contact between parties must be conducive to friendly interactions.
- **Typical contact:** The people that are met must be perceived as typical of the other groups, so that the positive perceptions are generalized to the rest of the population. This is important for the shattering of stereotypes and the gradual shift away from kneejerk reactions.
- **Social norms of equality:** In the situation of contact, it must be a general norm that all parties are equal. If one side enjoys a perception of more privileges than the other all attempts at mediation are off.

What works in geo-political situations and conflict resolution scenarios can work in the market place.

How to Create a Trust-Regaining Strategy

Whether trust can be regained quickly or not, or at all, depends upon the severity of the crisis and the alleged offence that has caused the loss of trust to occur, the length and depth of the bond between a brand or a company and its audience, the previous history of the brand and the way that the crisis will be handled.

Anyone of course can regain trust provided they handle the situation correctly. Even Union Carbide did not have to go down, the way it did. Every trust-crisis that was handled successfully had eight specific steps in common. It is these that will form the basis of any strategy:

- **Assess the situation** – Don't panic and don't over-react. Collect all the data. Get specific, find out exactly what is happening, who the stakeholders are and what is the apparent cause of the issue. Focus on what is driving the story forward. Create a Timeline. Populate it properly with facts, as many as you can get, and constantly enrich it. Document your actions from the outset. If you haven't got a crisis-management protocol in place, meticulous documentation is the only safeguard you have of any accusation of a cover-up.

- **Determine the issue** – Not every crisis is about what it appears to be about. Collect everything you can but focus directly on the things that impact you. Don't look at the bottom line. That will always be affected. Focus instead on the real issues.

- **Set your priorities** – This is critical. The natural response of any brand or company under attack is to act to safeguard itself by acting defensively or denying any wrongdoing. Paradoxically that is exactly what will cause things to escalate and create further damage to the brand. Consider that in 1982 Johnson & Johnson was not at fault. Out of millions of sales it had just seven deaths and the issue was one of supermarket and warehouse storage security rather than the quality of its product, Tylenol. This is not how it approached it. It saw the issue as one of public health. The priority was to safeguard peoples' lives. The secondary concern was to save the product (and the company). The secondary concern was achieved because the Johnson & Johnson leadership determined the issue correctly and set the right priorities.

- **Open up a line of communication** – Companies under attack tend to huddle in their trenches. While behind the scenes they may be frantically striving to set things right, the outward appearance is that they don't care. This creates a perception of indifference that is fed by the general impression of the way companies act. Without a line of communication, this perception is aired, becomes a reality and when the company acts to address it, it is seen as further evidence of its culpability and defensiveness and it only adds to the building sense of mistrust.

- **Create transparency** – Don't do things behind the scenes in a silo, expecting the public to understand. Transparency is critical in re-establishing a human connection between a tainted brand and its

184

audience.

- **Lead the conversation** – Do not expect to be trusted again if all you do is react to the situation. The perception is that your hand is forced, rather than that you are making genuine efforts to set things right.

- **Humanize your efforts** – Nothing is done automatically, by robots from another galaxy. Go to great efforts to get a very human face in front that actually addresses your audience in a way they recognize and identify with.

- **Show results** – Nothing proves that things have changed more than tangible results people can see and feel and touch. Not every situation can be resolved quite so tangibly as the Tylenol tamper-proof bottle perhaps but every situation can bring about lasting change, striking a blow not just for the good of the brand or the company, but for the general good of the world. Show what has been learnt from the crisis, what you've done to make sure it doesn't happen again and how this benefits the world.

Remember brand trust may be part of an unwritten psychological contract that is primarily between a company and its audience but the whole world has a stake in trust and the moment it is jeopardized through the actions of an individual or a company, the whole world is quick to condemn the situation.

If you don't or cannot take all of these steps as you deal with your trust-crisis the odds of your brand or company making it through it, unscathed are small.

Summary

When trust is threatened between a brand or a company and its audience it threatens trust everywhere. Individual cases can easily escalate if left unaddressed. Companies can become beacons of hope, if their ethos and attitude are good or magnets for hate if they come to symbolize everything that is wrong with big business, corporations, capitalism and faceless processes.

Dealing with a loss of trust requires genuine communication, great humanization and a genuine desire to set things straight. Although each strategy applied will depend upon the severity of the crisis, they all have eight steps in common that need to be applied in order to resolve it.

Five Key Questions to Answer

1. How much goodwill does your brand or company have stored up, at the moment How do you measure it?

2. What is your crisis-management strategy? How does it stack up when compared with the eight steps you need to take to restore trust in your organization?

3. What steps do you have in place that humanize your business?

4. How do you communicate within your organization?

5. Looking at the examples we have covered so far identify the trust-building strategies employed by Starbucks, Amazon, John Lewis, Johnson & Johnson, Union Carbide. Be very detailed in your answers giving full justification.

Book III

Trust Flow
(how Trust propagates on the web)

"All the world is made of faith, and trust, and pixie dust."
J.M. Barrie, Peter Pan

1

The Web of Trust

As a psychosocial construct trust is a communal cognitive and affective response that, traditionally, has helped us survive. The communal threats these days may not be quite as life threatening but the need for trust is as important as ever. As the digital space is heading towards a semantic web can we hope to reach a level of transparency and connectivity that the online, connected, digital space becomes the village square of our more bucolic past? In this chapter we shall be looking at concepts such as algorithmic trust and the creation of trust networks in the digital space and how they affect us. What practical lessons can we draw from them?

W e live not just in the digital age but in the digital domain. Whether we like it or not our physical self has a digital doppelganger whose digital footprint can be traced from our Tweets about politics and the lunch we had today to our Facebook shares and LinkedIn articles to the Google+ interactions. As a matter of fact, we could argue that over time our digital self, stripped from many of the requirements of our flesh and blood existence that force to co-exist in social structures which we have not consciously chosen to be part of, is pure intentionality and therefore a truer picture of us.

If trust is the one constant, ubiquitous requirement for any type of relational exchange to take place how is it manifested in the digital space? What are the elements that make it strong or weak? Can it be manipulated? Is there such a thing as algorithmic trust? And if so, how is that even possible when trust is so precious and hard to obtain because it is, precisely, a very human emotion?

It is only natural that we start with questions. The digital realm is new to us still. We are still rapidly evolving in it and just when we think that we have got a handle on it, just when we feel that we understand what we are doing, we blink just a little longer and things change again, and we are, once more on a learning curve.

While the digital realm is characterized by incessant change and non-stop challenges, it is also rife with opportunities we have never had before. Made up of data it also transforms us into data. On the web we are nodes, our interactions and engagements become edges and the tensile strength between nodes and their relational connections to each other becomes an intricate pattern of nodes and edges whose numerical values, ever changing, tell a story of friendships, acquaintances, jobs, careers, hobbies, likes, dislikes and new discoveries.

In many ways the digital realm is pure magic. It is almost anything we could have ever wished for except for the fact that we are still struggling to understand it, its impact and out place in it. In the digital realm the story of trust is born anew and within it, we have the chance to get some things we messed up in the real world, right.

The Semantic Web and Calculation of Trust

We looked a little at algorithmic trust in the second section of this book in

Chapter four so here we are free to build on that foundation and actually explore things a little bit further. The ultimate dream of the semantic web is that it becomes a vast, transparent arena of connected data and people where one could digitally venture into any space with the same confidence that they leave their own front door in the morning.

"Lack of trust is one of the most frequently cited reasons for consumers not purchasing from Internet vendors" begins a detailed research paper on the subject that appears in the *International Journal of Human-Computer Studies*. It is a by now familiar tune. Written by researchers from the University of Klagenfurt in Austria, the paper cites one instance after another of online situations where trust is not present and online transactions do not take place, despite the fact that the tools to carry them out are all there.

> *"Trust, in general, is an important factor in many social interactions, involving uncertainty and dependency. Online transactions and exchange relationships are not only characterized by uncertainty, but also by anonymity, lack of control and potential opportunism, making risk and trust crucial elements of electronic commerce."*

Since the articulation of the Semantic Web vision, it has become the focus of research on building the next web. The philosophy behind the Semantic Web is the same as that behind the World-Wide Web: anyone can be an information producer or consume anyone else's information.

There are specific problems associated with that:

> *"One major difficulty is that, by its very nature, the Semantic Web is a large, uncensored system to which anyone may contribute."*

The problems presented by new technology usually have a technological solution to them, we just need to find it. Just one suggestion coming out of the IBM Almaden Research Center employs the measurement of personalized trust scores:

> *"One major difficulty is that, by its very nature, the Semantic Web is a large, uncensored system to which anyone may contribute. This raises the question of how much credence to give each source. We cannot expect each user to know the trustworthiness of each source, nor would we want to assign top-down or global credibility values due to the subjective nature of trust. We tackle this problem by employing a web of trust, in which each user*

maintains trusts in a small number of other users. We then compose these trusts into trust values for all other users. The result of our computation is not an agglomerate "trustworthiness" of each user. Instead, each user receives a personalized set of trusts, which may vary widely from person to person."

The approach suggested uses path algebra to calculate the strength and quality of the connection between a small set of people on the web. The idea behind it is that when a statement is made and another statement is derived from it, the trustworthiness of the original statement can be calculated based upon the trust values of the originating source and the group that source belongs to and this then allows a further calculation of trustworthiness to be made to the derivative statement. Do this across the web and you end up with cases where you have sufficient information to make a direct judgment call on trustworthiness and cases where you have just enough information to make a probabilistic judgment call on trustworthiness.

Here's what's at stake, which makes this approach as exciting as it is important:

- Identities
- Careers
- Online and offline business
- Personal finance
- Personal relationships

Already there are algorithms that are used to establish a personal trust score and determine the suitability of an individual for a loan. Already, an algorithm called Vital sits on the board of directors of deep Knowledge Ventures, a firm that focuses on drugs for age-related diseases. The algorithm looks at a range of data when making decisions - including financial information, clinical trials for particular drugs, intellectual property owned by the firm and previous funding.

This highlights an interesting problem we have not really had to address before: while we know that a machine can potentially do a specified job, tirelessly, without making mistakes and much faster than a human (which is why Vital sits on the board tasked with making very specific decisions), which are we predisposed to trusting: the algorithm or intuition?

The question brings into focus the way we use cognitive and affective trust to reach at decisions and the weight we are prepared to put on each part of trust in each instance. Of particular importance in this area is a study conducted of Uber drivers by researchers of the Human-Computer Interaction Institute, Carnegie Mellon University. Uber drivers basically interact with an app that is backed by a recommendation and reward algorithm. The algorithm determines specific driver ratings based on a specified set of statistics, determines rates and who will or will not get the chance to pick up a ride. In addition it provides informational support and evaluates the driver's job performance.

What is striking in that study is that the app interface becomes the contact point between a human and an algorithm and trust from the human develops in the same way that it would had it been a human-to-human contact. Namely:

- Creating workaround strategies for perceived algorithm deficiencies
- Acquiring information in online forums (since corporate communication in this context was non-existent) to determine how to sync best with the way the algorithm works
- Sensemaking through an online Uber drivers support network
- Seamlessly mixing their own experience with the information the algorithm provided to maximize the efficiency of each assigned ride

What came across most clearly was that those drivers who were savvy enough to go online and acquire a little bit of knowledge of the strengths and limitations of the algorithm they worked with, through online forums, also reported the best work experience.

In the semantic web online businesses that want to create a trust-inspiring environment need to work at employing a specific set of steps:

- Create an information-rich environment both in and outside the business. Make sure there is enough information on your website for visitors to do their own due diligence and that information is easy to find and straightforward to understand (for instance a returns policy full of clauses and legalese may cover the requirement of having one but will not inspire confidence).
- Create transparency in how the business operates. Values, ethos, motivation and overall belief system.

- Create a reputation across the web. Find your audience and engage with them in an identification-based way. You can't be on sales-mode all the time.

- Humanize your business. Think what is important to your target audience and work hard to make sure it is provided.

- Build relationships based on cognitive trust. Carefully itemize the direct benefits your business provides and make sure it meets them.

- Build relationships based on affective trust. If there is no emotional connection between your business and its customers, they are not really your customers.

The online and offline environments are converging through the use of mobile devices and the presence of reputation systems like Yelp and Trip Advisor that bridge the online and offline worlds and drive reputation-based trust in both.

Think of the relationship you want to build with your customers first and the outcome you want to achieve as a result and the technology second. The technology will evolve and change, again and again. The kind of relationships you establish with your customers and the way you work in your business shouldn't.

Creating Trust Networks

We talk about social networks and digital platforms spring to mind like Facebook and Twitter, Google+ and LinkedIn, Instagram and Pinterest. They differ in functionality as well as demographics and even their intent and purpose are different so it is good to actually define what it is, exactly, that we mean with the words "social network".

First coined by the social anthropologist, John Barnes in 1954, in the article "Class and Committees in a Norwegian Island Parish" a social networks is represents relationships and flows between people, groups, organizations, computers or other information/knowledge processing entities. The activity that occurs within a social network is usually expressed through the topological mathematics of graph theory where the words `connectedness' and `connectivity' may refer to properties of the distance between persons, the number of paths between them, whether there is a path at all, or the proportion of possible paths actually in existence.

Simplified a little a social network is a grouping of people drawn to it by a broadly common purpose defined by the network's intent and connected through several degrees of separation that are determined by how close their particular experiences and interests are.

Barnes, in what must have been a moment of epiphany, thought that the edges in a network represent interdependencies between nodes so that they could be: interactions, invitations, trades, values, and so on. While social networks like Google+, Facebook and even MySpace are global in nature and massive in size but still work according to small-group dynamics where people make personal connections in them based upon their sense of affinity for other members of the network. But that is not the whole picture.

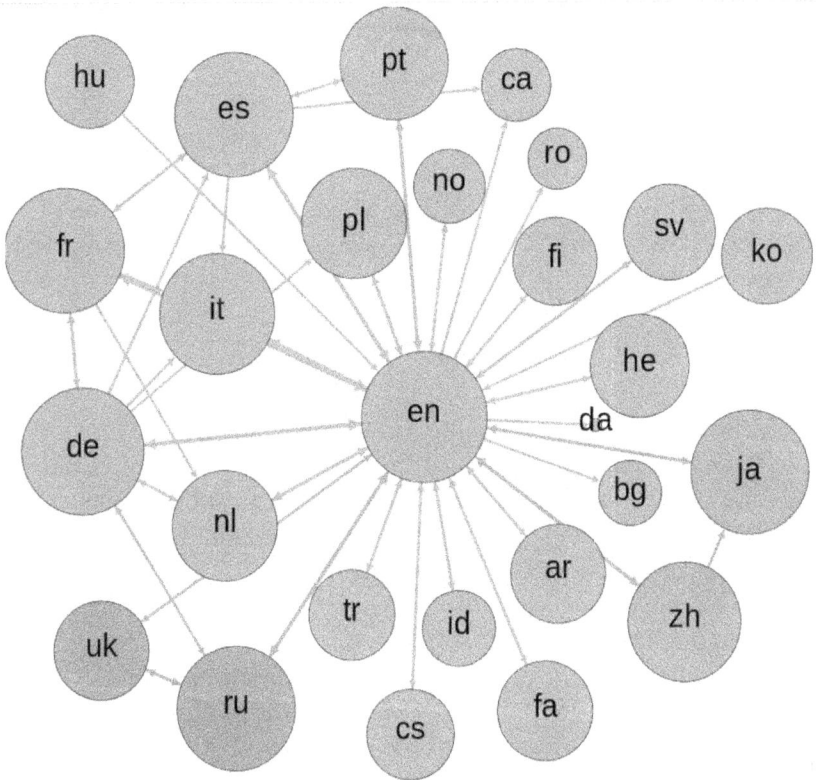

Fig 1.1 - *The network graph formed by Wikipedia editors (edges) contributing to different Wikipedia language versions (vertices) during one month in summer 2013 (some rights reserved Wikipedia)*

Network connections exist because the network environment itself always has a trust mechanism in place. The social-network-based method of assessing trust uses social relationships to rank nodes (i.e. people) in the network. While this may be done in any number of ways within the network itself in order to help the network administrators determine the value of content and the focus of activity of network members, it also happens at the human level in an ad hoc way, through the observation of specific social proof elements like popularity of a person posting, recognition, familiarity with other members, perceived authority and so on.

Within a social network setting trust is a measure of confidence that an entity will behave in an expected manner, despite the lack of ability to monitor or control the environment in which it operates. Social networks usually provide some form of deterrent that includes reporting bad behavior to network administrators and/or blocking a person from having any other interaction with members who are find his behavior causing unnecessary friction.

There are two key concepts that anyone with an online business needs to keep in mind. The first is that clustering within a social network (grouping which can include communities, posts or groups) occurs along two distinct types:

- **Homophily** – There are two distinct types of that status homophily, which is based on ascribed status such as race, ethnicity, age, religion, education, occupation, and so on, and value homophily which is based on values, attitudes, and beliefs, that is, a tendency to associate with others who think in similar ways, regardless of differences in status. Depending on the type of social network or even the type of clustering that occurs within it, there can be an overlap in these two types of homophily so that status-based categorization may also bring people together who share similar ideas.
- **Small-world phenomenon** - there are two different views on the "small world" phenomenon in social networks. Stanley Milgram, the original developer of the "small-world problem", famously popularized the notion of there being "six degrees of separation" between any two people in the world. Later experiments involving computer networks later investigated the "small-world problem" in the modern computerized world, where small world networks were assumed to be everywhere (e.g., online social networks; email networks; networks of movie stars, boards of directors, and scientists; neural networks; genetic regulatory networks, protein interaction

networks, metabolic reaction networks; World Wide Web; food Webs; and so on). The view is that instead of being one highly connected small world, our world consists of many loosely connected and some disconnected small worlds.

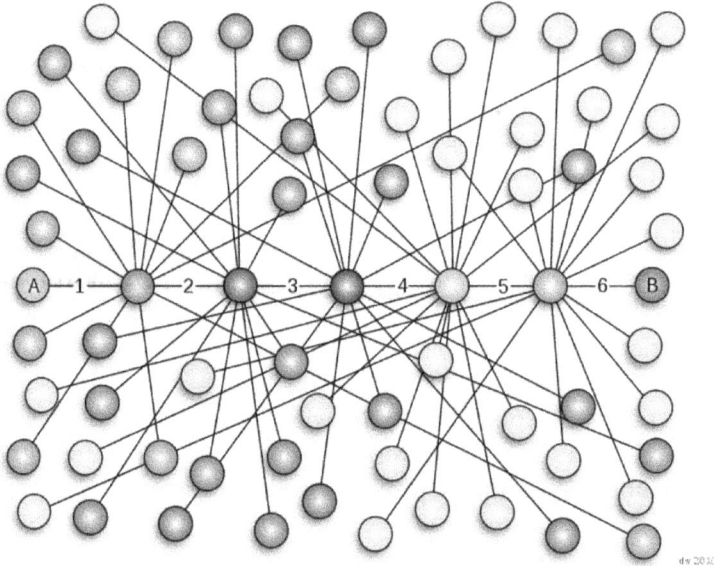

Fig 1.2 - *"Six degrees of separation" by Daniel' (User:Dannie-walker) - Own work. Licensed under CC BY-SA 3.0 via Commons - https://commons.wikimedia.org/wiki/ File:Six_degrees_of_separation.svg#/media/*

Homophily and the small-world phenomenon where the Friend-of-a-Friend (FOAF) concept occurs make it possible to generate trust quickly by association. The underlying assumption behind this concept is that the relation "friendship" is transitive. The foundation of every friendship is trust and in a social network setting trust is propagative rather than transitive, spreading along the connections between nodes (people), its quality and endurance dependent upon the strength of the edges (connections) that form between them.

Social networks render the problem of how a business can scale being personal, solvable. Suppose you are looking for a car to buy and you already have a general specification and price range in mind, you're faced with the problem of now having to do a considerable amount of work to narrow down all the available choices to you and then convince yourself of the final decision you've made.

The natural shortcut here is to ask your friend network for a recommendation that will point you in the right direction. A car dealership that is successful at forming trustworthy relationships could benefit from a recommendation in this context, finding prospects and customers without having to resort to expensive advertising or hard-sell techniques.

One organization who has spent a lot of time looking at trust and online sales for automakers is DrivingSales. As Fig 1.3 shows, the influence of friends and family feature heavily amongst the factors that lead a prospect to a particular car dealership.

Had the vehicle I was interested in listed on their website

Read positive customer reviews online

Was the closest dealership with the brand I'm interested in

Had the vehicle I was interested in in stock

Convenient location

REASONS SHOPPERS CONTACT DEALERSHIP?

Past experience with dealership

Only nearby dealership with the brand I am interested in

Saw a positive post on Facebook

Family member recommended dealership

Dealership had a "Request a Price Quote" form on their website

Friend recommended dealership

DrivingSalesUniversity.com

DrivingSales2015

Fig 1.3 – *Original research carried out by DrivingSales showed that car dealership recommendation by friends and family was the strongest of three group factors affecting a car buyer's decision.*

When it comes to using social media to increase brand awareness traditional marketers balk at the investment of time and effort required because there is no direct return-on-the-investment (ROI) metric they can apply that will show a bottom line advantage.

Yet, social media engagement allows a conversation to take place where brand values and brand ethos can be shared without the added pressure of selling, which lead to brand trust which has both a brand equity and a bottom line in terms of market share impact. We live in an age where we don't trust brands, companies or corporations just because they tell us to. We need to feel we can connect with them and understand them under our own actions, not their instigation. We need to feel that we like them because we want to, not because their advertising slogans tell us how likable they are.

Those companies that don't get this, brands that don't understand it and corporations that do not respect it are on a downward value spiral from which they may never recover.

Summary

Trust is also present in the digital environment. Social networks propagate trust so that brands, business and companies that enjoy a good reputation in one part of the network soon find themselves discovering new friends and new potential customers.

While there is no direct impact of social media brand-awareness and trust-building activity to a company's sales, it is a fact that without trust nothing will happen. No sales, no contact, not even a phone call. Many companies fail to understand the need to build a trust bank. They still rely on brand equity the old-fashioned way forgetting that relationships take time and the older they are the more valuable and more robust they become.

Five Key Questions to Answer

1. Name five things that you believe drive your company's, brand's or organization's reputation.
2. Give clear explanations of the pathway that brings customers to you.
3. Explain in detail what you think your social media presence does for your company, brand or organization.
4. Do you have examples of recommendation that lead to sales for your company, brand or organization? Be very specific.
5. Explain how you hope to take advantage of the small-world phenomenon to increase the impact of your brand. Be specific and explain every step of your strategy.

2

Trust and the Social Network

Social networks are a challenge. They are a social construct made up of people and their interactions, running on technological platforms that are governed by algorithms. They are a conceptual space where the essence of what it means to be human interacts seamlessly with what a machine is designed to do best. Trust is as important in cyberspace as it is in the offline world we live in. Like most human qualities it can be broken down into distinct, measurable steps which allow it to acquire a calculable value. In this chapter we shall see that as the online and offline world merge trust and trustworthiness in one begins to translate into the same qualities in the other. We may not quite feel it ourselves but we are actually already living in cyberspace, our selves and activities already divided in corporeal and digital avatars, working with intent.

We use tools to facilitate relationships. This is hardly news. The Victorians managed to do the equivalent of texting using the penny post (which they invented) to communicate on specific subjects, starting conversations that went on for months. They gave us, in the process, the epistolary novel which is an acknowledgment that any conversation has a beginning, middle and end punctuated by highs and lows. Their letters often became volumes of works that reflected the exploration of a subject, two questing minds, writing their thoughts to each other, building on each other's ideas to seek a higher place of understanding.

One could not read *The Collected Letters of Thomas and Jane Carlysle* without feeling that they were eavesdropping in the mental processes of two great thinkers struggling with the role of language in literature and communications. The world has become smaller and more transparent because we strive to break out of our isolation, our brains seek to connect with others and in the connection we find both a sense of wonder and fulfillment.

The seeming cacophony of 'LOLs', cat-picture shares, memes being passed along and holiday pics being shared forms an ever increasingly dense backdrop of human-to-human communication taking place via social media platforms. With more and more powerful devices, extended points of access and more of us online, it seems that the more isolated we are the more connected we become. The more connected we want to be and the more we feel the need for "the human touch".

The importance of this becomes evident when we take into account a new Pew Research report titled "Teens, Technology, and Romantic Relationships" which shows that:

- For boys who were dating, 65% said social media made them more connected to a significant other while it was 52% for girls

- 50% of all teens surveyed, dating or not, said they had indicated interest by friending someone on Facebook or other social media and 47% expressed attraction by likes and comments

- Texting is king - 92% of teens who were dating said they texted a partner, assuming the partner would check in with "great regularity"

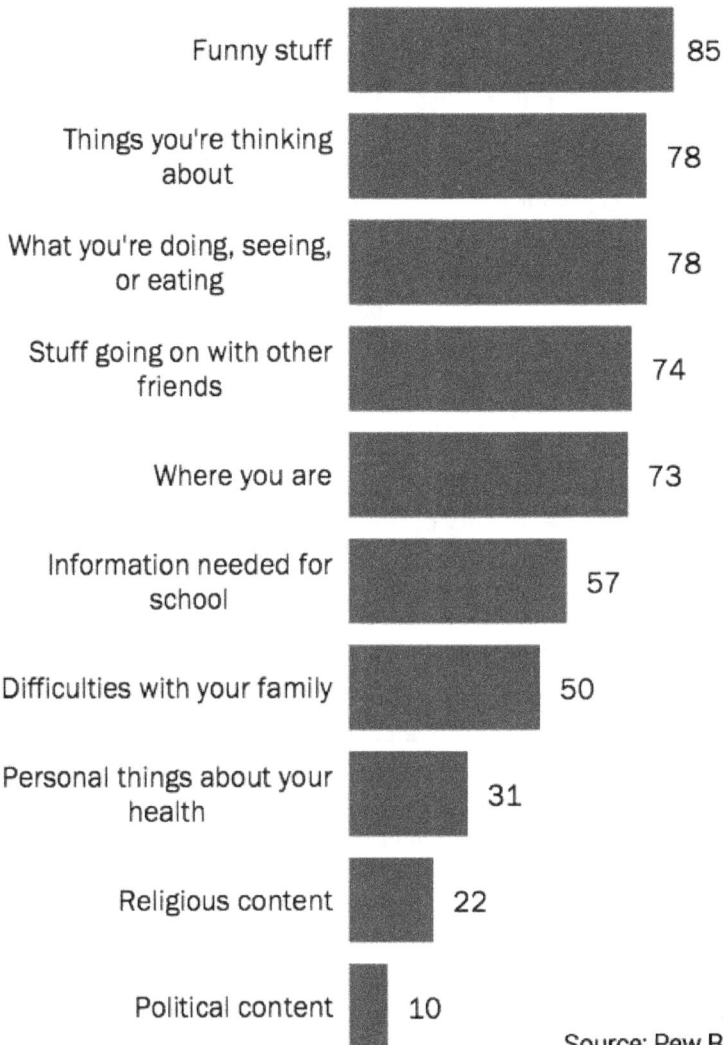

Funny stuff	85
Things you're thinking about	78
What you're doing, seeing, or eating	78
Stuff going on with other friends	74
Where you are	73
Information needed for school	57
Difficulties with your family	50
Personal things about your health	31
Religious content	22
Political content	10

Source: Pew Research

Fig 2.1 – *The Pew Research report shows that teens are quick to make use of technology to stay connected.*

Technology is making many of the scary parts of that first connection between humans, easier and way less scary. Trust, in that context then begins to form gradually and get tested constantly not unlike it would have in our ideal scenario of a medieval village.

Social networks, unsurprisingly, are changing even the way we think about trust and this is where a fresh paradox arises. As in everything humans drive the connection. Our actions, interactions, posts, comments, shares, re-shares, +1s, Likes and thumb ups, become part of the human behavior that says something about that particular instant in time and the piece of content over which all this is happening. By association they also say something about ourselves, the content sharer and everyone else who may have engaged on that particular topic or thread. While all this is human, the activity we engage in is also visible to machines.

Algorithms look at individual user profiles, mine the connections between them, check for patterns, historical behavior, subject matter expertise, close or distant affiliation and then determine a trust score for the content, the person, the subject matter and everything associated with them. This, in turn, determines visibility, importance and relative trustworthiness.

Trust, in a social network environment, because of our interactions morphs from the ethereal, elusive quality of the early days of trust research into something more tangible, more concrete. A quality that has a numerical value and many small but visible moving parts, each of which signifies something to a machine that can read it, measure it and faithfully record it.

The opening paragraph on a paper from a team of University College London researchers, in England, states the challenge quite well:

> "Using mobile devices, such as smart phones, people may create and distribute different types of digital content (e.g., photos, videos). One of the problems is that digital content, being easy to create and replicate, may likely swamp users rather than informing them. To avoid that, users may organize content producers that they know and trust in a web of trust. Users may then reason about this web of trust to form opinions about content producers with whom they have never interacted before. These opinions will then determine whether content is accepted. The process of forming opinions is called trust propagation."

The traditional approach of assigning a value of trust to a web resource according to a centralized global arbiter was something Google did with the visible part of PageRank on websites. The little green bar of a rating from one to 10 was intended, primarily for website visitors looking for some way to determine the credibility of a website and it worked, for a while. The fact that Google gradually retired it in 2013 by not putting out any more updates is an indication of the fresh difficulties faced in a semantic web overseen by semantic search where the speed at which information is shared and the different ways it has of being repurposed are a challenge.

As a matter of fact in real life we often wrestle with the problem of personalized trust where two people who know each other well, have a different opinion about the trustworthiness of a third individual whom they both know. The solution proposed by researchers is a variation of the small-world phenomenon we discussed in chapter 1 of this section of the book. Its basis is fairly simple, if personalized trust is something that varies between two individuals and depends on the strength of their connection, if we could assess all individuals on a relative basis then those who are most trustworthy are known then most because more people quote them, believe in them, think about them and are influenced by them. This is a little like PageRank for people, determined by machines.

Indeed, the researchers wrote:

> *"...on a graph in which: not links but nodes are either rated or unrated, and those nodes are then connected to each other if they are related (the techniques consider that two nodes are related if their ratings are similar). Informally, these techniques exploit knowledge already present in the graph (rated nodes) to construct a function that is capable of predicting unrated nodes."*

So, if George knows Tom and both believe that Nick is 100% trustworthy when Nick introduces Harry to the network Harry will enjoy a trust score (and a real perception of trust) even though he is totally unknown.

Influencer Marketing, Trust and Social Media

This is what brands and marketers look for, of course, when they tap into influencer marketing, seeking to take advantage of the power of established relationships of trust between a power user in a social network and his audience and gain acceptance and visibility.

That model worked well enough in the pre-social media world when banks would hire well-known actors to sell their brand in TV and magazine adverts, banking (as it were) on the popularity of the person they hired to personalize their brand and help it reach its audience.

The difference between then and now lies in connectivity. In that one-to-many way of communicating the message was fixed and the channel was top-down. In the transparency created by connectivity not only do we see the message and can challenged it but the response to the challenge is also visible and becomes part of the conversation. When the way something is done is as visible as what it is that was done, what surfaces in the transparency that results from it all, is a clearer understanding of values and motives. In other words, intent.

A brand that says still "Trust us, because of who we are" and leaves it at that, is unlikely to receive, in this environment, the welcome it hopes for.

Influencers can, then become, handy mediators. But does it work? It does if there is a real, relationship with real value between a brand, a power user and his audience. Even power users care about the connections they make in a social network setting, irrespective, of the large number of other users those connections may be with. Malcolm Gladwell's popular book *The Tipping Point* studies the way information flows are mediated by the networks of people and their associated trust relations:

> *"To be someone's best friend requires a minimum investment of time. More than that, though, it takes emotional energy. Caring about someone deeply is exhausting."*

We get down to the available amount of energy left to do anything with again. In chapter two of the second section of this book we saw just how trust allows us to function more cost-effectively by simplifying the world we live in and making our decision-making process easier.

In his book, *Thinking, fast and slow* American psychologist Daniel Kahneman showed how the incremental value assigned by people to transacting with a trusted party, affects people's beliefs and decision making. This suggests that the moment we are in a social network setting we are already deeply engaged in its trust calculation mechanism, our very human actions and reactions, become seamlessly embedded in the algorithmic process that underpins the platform we are on.

Our Facebook interactions and engagement, for instance, begins to coalesce into nodes we call "family" and "friends". Our engagement with or consumption of information, news, pictures, videos and memes becomes a vote of confidence towards people, companies and brands we trust. Suddenly, the online world we used to run to, to get away from reality and be irresponsible, is now every bit as important in the creation and propagation of trust as the offline world we are part of.

This makes us all responsible. Our online behavior, interactions, content consumption and content creation generate signals that affect the visibility of content and the popularity of other people and brands.

If you are running an online business the ingredients are simple:

- **Value** – make sure your content creation strategy produces something that's of use to most of your audience. This means that a mix of informational and practical posts are necessary. Aim for the core of your audience but don't be afraid to expand the reach.
- **Values** – create context for what you curate and/or share. Explain why it's important and show that what you do fits into a wider picture of activity that's informed by a broader set of values that your audience can understand, identify with and get behind. These are gateways to conversation and engagement, they become the bridging points that allow greater consideration of what your business does.
- **Tone** – your business may be a small family based operator or a large global conglomerate. Unless you show that it has a human face and a human voice that can approach its audience at their level, on things that are important to them, it will fail to resonate sufficiently to capture their attention.
- **Knowledge** – whatever you may do, however you may do it, if you are doing it well it has its own exceptional wealth of knowledge to impart. Knowledge shared is a key that helps unlock the context of your content and help gain attention.

Relationships Matter

The automatic calculation of trust in social network settings is, of course, in the first instance a classic case of Knowledge Based Trust (KBT) which we examined in more detail in chapter 3 of the second section of this book. But it's more than just that. While the algorithms use criteria such as, for instance, comment frequency and comment length, number of commenters on a thread, frequency of engagement between commenters, degree of interaction between commenters, domain expertise of commenters, network of friends of commenters, commenting history of each commenter in general, in an almost infinite degree of granularity, in order to establish the context, relevance and importance of a piece of content, what drives the initial interaction that sparks off all that activity is very much personal trust driven by more human traits: interests, relationships, passion, understanding, likes and dislikes.

The best piece of content in the world shared by someone whose avatar picture we dislike throws up a dissonance inside our heads that we find difficult to overcome. The most intelligent comment possible, dressed with four-letter expletives and pointed directly at us, will fail to find appreciative space inside our heads. The connections we make are still human after all. The systems we create are a hybrid of human and machine – a union intended to make a digital platform scale.

We have had scaling before. All the 20th century was devoted to the industrialization and scaling of processes that took a human activity, made it machine-reproducible and stripped the humanity out of it until we found ourselves living in a world where "trust" was a notion we paid lip service too. It put us on a slippery slope where we soon found ourselves paying lip service to other human notions too like "honesty", "honor" and "respect".

"Respect, Integrity, Communication and Excellence." Screamed Enron's motto at us. Its mission statement spelled out that "We treat others as we would like to be treated ourselves....We do not tolerate abusive or disrespectful treatment. Ruthlessness, callousness and arrogance don't belong here." - Yeah, right.

We saw in chapter two of the second section of this book that the moment respect is taken out of the equation trust fails to find foothold. We are, at the moment, facing a unique challenge: How do we make relationship marketing that's best suited to a medieval village square setting, scale? We are also faced with a unique opportunity: Make relationships matter and we achieve a degree of authenticity that automatically increases trust in the world we live in and its evolution.

That is about as good a win-win scenario as it can get.

Summary

The perception that trust is a difficult thing to attain or obtain in a digital setting is patently false. Because we are more intently focused in what we are doing and our intent is clearer in the digital space, it becomes easier to create trusting relationships and trusted networks. The moment we venture into cyberspace we become part of a human-machine hybrid where both our humanity and our sense of trust are manifested and instantly matter to both a digital platform's algorithms and its human population.

Five Key Questions to Answer

1. How do you generate genuine engagement in your social media presence? Discuss this in detail and give examples of instances where this has worked and where this has failed.

2. How human is your social media posting? Explain your social media strategy and how this helps you promote the core values of your company, or brand. Be very precise and detailed, explain the connection between the subjects you post about and the tone you use and the core values and beliefs of your organization.

3. What more could you do to humanize your brand?

4. How do you make sure that the relationships you form online matter? Give specific examples of how you achieve that as an individual, a company or a brand.

5. What is the key to your social media activity? What is the specific direction that guides it across all digital platforms? Give a detailed answer that explains your philosophy when it comes to social media engagement.

3

The Future of Trust

Trust succeeds in challenging us all. Artists and writers working as a brand suddenly find themselves having to build a real trust with their audience. Brands, companies and businesses of all types, are struggling to get their personality across, define exactly what it is they stand for and how best to show it. The requirement of trust that is necessitated by the very human connections made across an increasingly transparent, very mobile and very voluble we is managing to throw everyone equally. In this, final chapter of the book, we shall see exactly why this challenge is happening, how trust is, once again, key and we will also look at the future of trust, not so much as an evolving quality, because it isn't but as an increasingly key ingredient in a world where complexity is escalating.

Here's a thought experiment. You've spent months agreeing a multi-million dollar deal with a wealthy partner. You have agonized over the stipulations of the contract and the conditions you feel are necessary to make the deal worth your while. You now present it all in a 100-page contract. You're in a room, sitting down, facing each other.

Your future business partner goes carefully through the contract and then goes ahead and signs every single page, agreeing to every one of your terms and conditions. The meeting is a success. A glorious, mutually beneficial enterprise lies ahead for the both of you. Business concluded and contract signed, you stand up and offer to shake hands across the table. Your business partner also stands up, looks at your extended hand, and then simply turns around and walks out of the room.

Do you trust him to hold up his end of the bargain in the contract he just signed?

By now, of course, having go this far in the book you are wiser. You know that while you and your prospective business partner both agreed to the cognitive trust part of your deal, because as business people you are both rational animals, the affective component of trust is simply not there. At a human level you both distrust each other.

The gesture of a handshake is a very human one. Humanizing any kind of contact is exactly what trust is designed to do. A study on evolution and human behavior carried out by researchers from the Center for Neuroeconomics Studies, Claremont Graduate University, the Division of Dermatology, School of Medicine, University of California, and the Department of Neurology, Loma Linda University Medical Center, all of them in California, found that:

> *Humans frequently sacrifice resources to help others—even strangers. The proximate mechanisms inducing such sacrifices are not well understood, and we hypothesized that touch might provoke a sacrifice of money to a stranger. We found that touch significantly elevated circulating oxytocin (OT) levels but only when it was followed by an intentional act of trust. Touch followed by trust increased monetary sacrifice by 243% relative to untouched controls. We also found that women were more susceptible than men to OT release and monetary sacrifice after touch. This suggests that touch draws on physiologic mechanisms that support cooperative behaviors in humans.*

We already know the benefits of touch from our own anecdotal experience.

We also know that touch implies trust. To even allow someone to come so close to us physically as to touch us, presupposes a degree of trust that they will not suddenly turn hostile and attack us.

We've already seen that we're wired to trust more than distrust. Trust makes life easier. Distrust complicates things. This, suggests Paul Zak, who is the founding Director of the Center for Neuroeconomics Studies and Professor of Economics at Claremont Graduate University, makes us easy to con. To prove it Zak and his research team run complex, well thought-through experiments in their lab where they con unsuspecting subjects.

Zak (who's also the author of *The Moral Molecule*) is a great believer in the way our predisposition to trust and our willingness to live in a less complicated world make us easy marks, but that is not quite right. Yes, we do want to trust and yes we'd rather take a risk and believe in a world that's essentially good than be rationally safe and believe that the world is the kind of place we simply don't want to be in, but unless we are targeted specifically by an expert con running a system, most of us are inoculated against cons.

Our brains do see the red flags. We do get uneasy when things appear "too good to be true", we do have doubts when a con is in play. What usually makes them work is the fact that we tend to keep quiet because we are isolated or because we think our fears are unfounded and voicing them will make us look both suspicious and foolish.

Being able to speak up like this requires a small support network. A safe harbor where some of the people around you, at least, are prepared to withhold judgment and simply listen. Do social media networks provide that for us? I would argue they do (or at the very least should) provided we do our job right and actually create the small networks of trust we need in order to navigate the world.

We are very good at doing this, in a small scale, in real life. That is our real superpower and the survival traits thousands of years of evolution have given us. We should be just as good at doing it in the digital domain where the safeguards in making new connections are actually even higher and where trust can be measured both at a cognitive and affective level. Nothing however runs on autopilot any more. The need for clear, analytical thinking and thoughtfulness is greater than ever.

Businesses Need to Adapt

Trust flows from one individual to another. That's how friendships are formed. It then, by association and recommendation flows on to other people, businesses, institutions, governments and countries. It adds value not by making relational exchanges easier but by making them possible. Relational exchanges lead to connections and connections lead to relationships and relationships add value to the world. Google happened because Larry Page met Sergey Brin. Could either have done it on his own? Maybe. Maybe not. But how different would the world be if they hadn't met?

As the world becomes more personal and personalized, as increasingly, smart algorithms, like Amazon's, make our experiences feel smooth, unforced, whisper-quiet and frictionless, trust and a sense of the human touch become important. Amazon does it at scale, putting tremendous thinking behind the approach, its impact and feel. Apple does it through the design of its products, the way the system works, how reliable it is and how it makes the user feel. Google does it by putting the person in the center, giving him total control and providing an experience that will make him stay and use more of Google's services.

These are massive, global tech companies dealing with millions of customers yet their approach and the pressures they face are no different to John Lewis ins the UK, where the personal touch is key to the in-store experience but which also deal with millions of customers every week. The point is that the 'system' we put in place is not the experience. Trust does not necessarily require human agency to occur. It requires a connection and an experience. A sense that someone, somewhere, actually thought about all this before it reached us.

A 2007 study from University of California, San Diego found that toddlers enjoyed playing with a two-foot tall human-like robot named QRIO who responded verbally when touched. Stanford University researchers reported that people who played online poker with a computer that cared about their wins and losses said they "trusted" the computer. And in the wildly popular massively multiplayer online games like Second Life, players routinely confuse others' avatars with the humans that control them.

In Japan, already there are service bots in some hotels and stores. The human/machine interface is about to get really complicated and the explosion in semantic technologies that has us interacting with weak forms of artificial intelligence (AI) is going to only increase the challenges, not make them fewer.

In all of this the businesses that will do well and thrive are those who will succeed in establishing a genuine, sincere connection with their customers and prospects. It will be the ones who no longer shout: "buy my stuff" but want to know "how can we help you?".

Because no matter how far and how fast technology evolves some things never change, there is a list of actionable points a business active in the world of today can use as a handy playbook:

1. What drives your business forward?
2. Who makes the decisions?
3. How do you make sure that everyone does what they should?
4. Where is the line drawn in your idealism?
5. What happens when what you do causes some kind of damage along the way?
6. What happens when a competitor goes after you with all guns blazing?
7. How do you keep your employees happy?
8. Where do all your new ideas come from?
9. How do you deal with the need for change in your organization?
10. How do you deal with failure in your organization?

Within these ten questions lie hidden changes that need to be made, work that needs to be done and repositioning both within and without the business boundaries, that needs to be undertaken.

The future of trust is personable. It will always be so irrespective of whether we interact with our cars (themselves becoming AI-enhanced mobile, cognitive computing platforms), the smart cities that are coming, the robot revolution that is round the corner and the explosion of intelligent bots that will talk to us like they are people.

The web has always been a publishing medium. As a matter of fact it's the effect it had on the democratization of publishing that allowed ordinary people to produce content at will that has been a catalyst to dramatic change on many fronts.

When citizen-journalism is possible and content can be produced by anyone with a blog, a web cam and a digital camera (in any combination of the three) the gatekeeper role of content creators such as newspapers, magazines, big publishers and large organizations becomes redundant. When content is created by so many, so fast, in so many different ways, indexing it requires more than just the ability to catalogue it. It needs context, importance, relevance and trustworthiness.

The wave of content that led to the explosion of Big Data on the web, became the reason that led us to semantic search. A clever means of organizing massive amounts of data so they do not overwhelm us, semantic search (search, really, as semantic technology is powering almost every search engine) also changed the way we view the veracity of content. Used to taking advertising at face value, our response to it highly dependent on the inclusion of emotional triggers (playing heavily on our fears, concerns and worries) we now want content to talk to us using our language, addressing our real concerns, appealing to logic as well as emotion and connecting with us as real people, rather than faceless units in a potential audience addressed en-masse by a cleverly crafted marketing message.

Branding, marketing, search engine optimization and content creation, then stopped being separate disciplines in the marketing toolbox, only passingly acknowledging each other. In the 21st century they have become a unified means of addressing the needs of the audience and a direct way of making contact with them.

A recent study by Chartbeat on the online news media data metrics showed that:

> *"About 40% of visitors leave having spent fewer than 15 seconds engaged on the page — and yet the pageview is often viewed as the most important metric.*
>
> *It's not enough to get someone to click. We have to get them to read."*

Chartbeat provides editorial reporting to 80 per cent of the leading digital publishers in the US, and in a further 60 countries globally, using its publishing tools to help editorial staff create engaging content and design sites so its statistics are based on sufficient data to sound a warning bell.

Online news sites of course don't just serve news. They also serve ads and it is these that the statistic posted above is actually killing. When the news content you create is barely sufficient to stop the eye for 15 seconds, you can guarantee that no one is looking at the ads you charge clients, to place on the site.

The fact that attention and engagement are better metrics than pageviews has led the Interactive Advertising Bureau's European body to urge adoption of viewability as the basis for display ad transactions, giving a virtual greenlight for publishers and advertisers to start using 'attention' as a significant advertising currency.

This is where trust comes in. News and content become compelling when it comes from a trustworthy source, has something relevant to say and presents it in a way that is very accessible. Making readers jump through hoops by separating a 500 word article into four pages so you can serve more ads and more pageviews (as an example) is neither the best way to grab their attention nor gain their trust.

So, what works?

- **Transparency** – by all means serve your needs as a publisher, eCommerce website, marketer but also acknowledge the fact that you care about your readers. Work hard to show you do. No one says business should not work hard to make money, but a business that resorts to the online equivalent of 'dirty tricks' in order to do so, fails to gain the respect of the audience it seeks to attract.

- **Vulnerability** – if you're running a site you really need people to get there. Acknowledge that, then work to make their time on your site as productive as possible even to your own detriment. If an article can deliver its content in 200 words, beefing it up to 800 is a disservice to the reader. Yes, you want them to stay on your site and yes you want them to remember you and come back. Treat them like you would yourself. It's the only way to gain trust and attention.

- **Value** – Stop producing content for content's sake. Yes, the web has turned us all into publishers but the content we produce now needs to truly work to justify the time it has taken to create. So take pride in your work, create content that says: "I am pouring my soul into this because I think it really matters" and then let your online audience do the rest.

- **Stop begging** – Sites that ask you to share their content with action calls that actually say "Share this with all your friends" may feel clever because they are ticking the "call to action" box in creating content, but they are also annoying the hell out of those who want to make up their own mind on what to share and what not to. This includes those annoying pop ups that always have the equivalent of "Do the clever thing and subscribe to our newsletter/RSS/mailing list" in big red letters while smaller bold font gives you the option of saying: "I want to remain uninformed/stupid/in the dark" and not subscribe to whatever they're offering. Really, that is so transparent it really turns people off.

- **Start leading** – Don't wait for people to find your site. Lead the online conversation on the issues that truly matter to your business by starting it, first. At the end of the day it is your business. If you don't care enough to raise your voice, who will?

The very recent (and at the moment of writing still far from over) crisis in the EU over Greece, logically should never have happened. All parties wanted the same thing: a stable Europe and a strong Euro, thriving membership economies that make EU membership even more attractive. What they got is so far from that, that you have to wonder why.

The answer, of course, lies where answers always lie when the stakes are high: personalities and personal visions, agendas and personal beliefs. The all too-human factor that makes it next to impossible to deal with the world and its many crises points, algorithmically.

As technology becomes more pervasive, as big data and analytics factor more and more in evidence-based decision making, it is the human factor that emerges as the defining quality around which everything, ultimately revolves.

It sounds paradoxical but really it isn't. When you strip away everything that distracts us by automating it, passing its function to smart algorithms that are designed to learn and respond, what is left is the irreducible quality of 'us'. The things that cannot yet be computed, the elements that cannot yet be done by a machine. And that's exactly where business and politics, frequently fall down, faltering on the trust pyramid that requires four critical ingredients to fostering trust, in the first instance:

- Awareness

- Understanding
- Belief
- Action

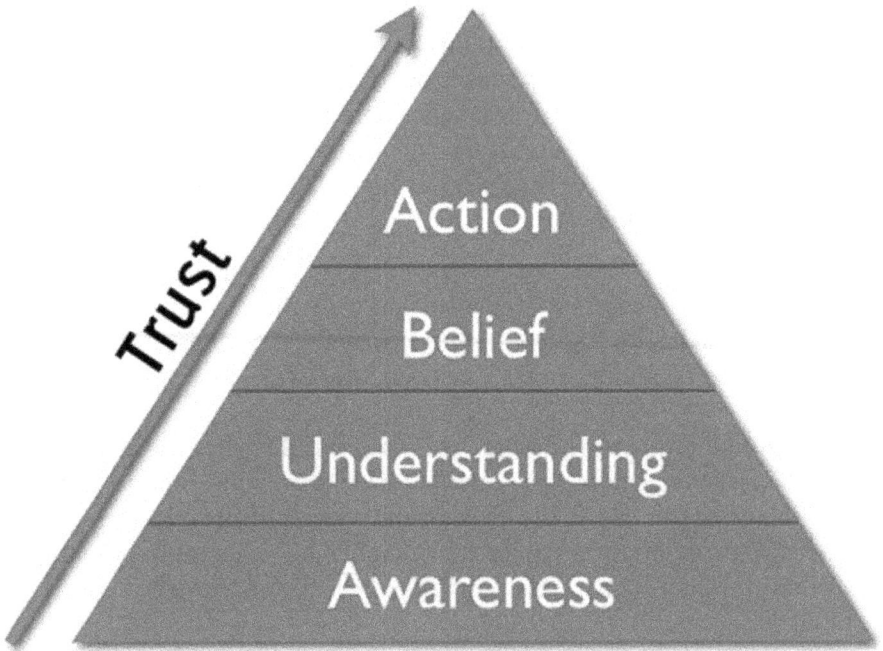

Fig 2.1 - *Without a way to establish a human factor in the connection with others, trust becomes difficult to establish.*

The fact that the US was able to make a satisfactory win-win deal with such a vastly different negotiator as Iran, over the contentious issue of nuclear capability and the EU couldn't agree on what it had to do to keep its house from collapsing point to systemic faults driven by the human factor.

The US deal was driven by professional diplomats whose stake was in getting a favorable outcome, the EU one was riven by politicians playing to their home, voter base and intent on saving face and scoring points.

If there is a lesson here to be drawn it has to be that in the machine learning age, where everything that is not yet automated and smart data analysis driven, soon will be, what we really value the most is what we have always had: the ability to connect on a one-to-one basis, build relationships, foster mutual understanding, use empathy, work together to overcome our differences and find ways to deliver mutual gains.

Summary

As the online population grows and the web becomes populated by more voices and more cultures trust is going to be more and more important at a conscious level. Trust algorithms may well become our line of first defense and there may well be apps where we shall be able to look up and get a first-hand approximation of a person's. business' or website's trustworthiness so that we can decide how high it should be on our priorities. In many ways the now retired public PageRank (PR) system of the past that Google used on websites was supposed to act a little like this.

Businesses, brands and individuals who do not heed the sea change and carry on like the world and the web are compartmentalized boxes will be faced with stark choices regarding their professional survival.

While mistakes can always happen and trust can be lost it can also be regained. It just takes a lot of effort to regain it.

Five Key Questions to Answer

1. If you were to put a dollar value to the trust your organization or brand enjoys right now, what would it be? Give specific explanations that show just how you arrived at that number.
2. What is your business' or brand's or organization's fallback strategy for rebuilding trust the moment there is an issue and it is threatened.
3. How does your website show visitors that you care?
4. What is the biggest challenge your business or organization face right now, regarding trust?
5. How transparent is your business, brand or organization. Give specific examples, explain the rationale behind them and also explain the effect you think this transparency has on your target audience. Again be specific.

The Last Word

Those familiar with my writing will know by now that my non-fiction books end on a personal note. In truth each one is a journey of sorts that allows me to pursue my interests and mine things from the world that are of direct value to me. This one is no exception.

The question of trust has been central in my thoughts ever since I was fifteen and it has been closely linked to my sense of identity. Moving countries often, as well as changing communities frequently, gave me the unenviable skill of forced adaptability. I found that I could easily assimilate the cultural paradigms of where I was, blending into the social fabric well enough to not stand out but never go deep enough to fully integrate.

That led to the question of who was I, exactly? From an ethnicity point of view was I Australian? Was I British? Did my time in the US and apparent ease of living there make me American? My professional life also raised questions. Was I a journalist who wrote books or a writer who wrote articles? Did my advisory capacity to global companies and large businesses make me a consultant or was I something else entirely? I will lie if I say that I have convinced myself that I know the answers to all of these questions.

While the rise of a global culture and a more connected, transparent world has given me much greater confidence in my sense of who I am and what it is that I actually do, trust in its broader sense and the way I have covered it in this book is a lot newer to me.

For a very large part of my life my personal conduct was guided by the admonition in Miyamoto Musashi's *Book of Five Rings* to "trust no one". Fully expecting those around me to let me down at some point (which they invariably did) the approach made me try harder to be better, smarter, stronger, more self-reliant and harder-working than anyone else. It might be perceived as a strength of sorts. It allowed me to become more analytical. It led me to habits of studying and learning which have really helped me in my professional life. It made me more disciplined in myself – qualities reflected in my focus on physical fitness that's been unwavering in my life despite any work or time-related challenges I face; and the value I place on doing what's right, even it if costs me personally. It also made me insular and lonely.

When you trust no one, you find yourself in the odd situation of being able to extend a measure of trust equally to everyone. Because you expect everyone to fail you it really does not matter if you really trust them or not.

So being judicious in how you apportion trust in that context is both futile and unnecessary.

The result of that approach created a deep disconnect within me that it took decades to resolve. As I struggled to change, my trusting people, openly, led to some unforeseen results. I experienced exemplary behavior from the most unlooked for quarters. I enjoyed complex, genuine ties with individuals and communities which, for parts of my life I gave 100% of myself to while expecting, fully at some point to simply move on, never look back.

Musashi, died on June 13, 1645, having lived his life alone, despite accolades, his final years were spent in a cave where he penned his treatise on swordsmanship, strategy and life. The legend surrounding him makes it hard to see the man underneath. Yet his admonition on trust and my later research on his upbringing allowed me to discern enough for me to be able to finally shake off the shackles of his teaching. As a man he was a failure. His passing through the world almost unnoticed. It was his writing of a slim treatise that saved him, raising his status to legendary heights while at the same time obscuring the lonely, mistrusting, ever alert and fearful individual who lay hidden beneath.

By choice, I've become more open in my dealings with others, more accepting of their failings and more willing to work to help them rectify mistakes and overcome weaknesses than at any other time in my life. I am now more willing to trust not just in eventual outcomes but also good intentions. In the process I have found myself having what I never had before. Friends, not acquaintances. A support network rather than a list of useful contacts. People I can talk to rather than talk at. Brains I can connect with rather than compete against. People whom I can respect rather than simply count as names on a list that makes up a community I am only passingly a member of. I have let myself depend on others and, to my surprise, they have rarely let me down and when they have, when they realized it, have worked hard to rectify things.

The result has accelerated my own growth and maturity and proved, to me at least, that it's never too late to rethink an approach. It has also vastly transformed my own life into one where I better understand what I do and who I do it for. It has given me a more, overall rewarding experience. To be clear, I changed. Things didn't.

Writing this book was not a revelation for me. It was the formalization of thoughts, beliefs, attitudes and concepts that I have been living for some years now. It is perhaps a book I should have written way sooner in my life. It might have led me to making better decisions at some critical points regarding relationships, it may have led to different career choices, I would certainly have taken some different paths. Every book though, like every thought, cannot be forced. It has to arise naturally out of the myriad underlying connections that become the stimuli which lead to its birth. It has to happen as part of real understanding of what's important and what isn't. There is no formula to authenticity. You know it because of the way it feels.

So this book. Now. Feels right.

Bibliography

Book 2

Chapter 1

J.K. Rowling, *Harry Potter and the Chamber of Secrets*, July 1st 1999 by Arthur A. Levine Books (first published 1998)

McKnight, Harrison D., Chervany, Norman, L., University of Minnesota Carlson School of Management.

Quotes About Trust, Goodreads, Goodreads Inc., https://www.goodreads.com/quotes/tag/trust

Quotes on Trust, Brainyquotes, Brainy Quotes Inc., http://www.brainyquote.com/quotes/topics/topic_trust.html

Trust, Inc, Inc., http://www.inc.com/lolly-daskal/trust-me-these-30-quotes-about-trust-could-make-a-huge-difference.html

Trust. "Definition", Oxford Dictionaries, Oxford University Press, http://www.oxforddictionaries.com/us/definition/american_english/trust

Chapter 2

Dunning D. et al, *Trust at zero acquaintance: more a matter of respect than expectation of reward*, American Psychological Association, 2014.

International Archives of Occupational and Environmental Health

Richard G. Peters, *A study of the factors determining perceptions of trust and credibility in environmental risk communication: the importance of overcoming negative stereotypes.*

OECD, *The Well-being of Nations The Role of Human and Social Capital: The Role of Human and Social Capital*, 2001.

The Real Story of the "Football" That Follows the President Everywhere, "Article", Michael Dobbs, Smithsonian, http://www.smithsonianmag.com/history/real-story-football-follows-president-everywhere-180952779

Park, Alice, *We Trust Strangers, Even When It Doesn't Make Sense to Do So*, Time, 16 May 2014.

Forward, S. (1989). *Toxic parents: Overcoming their hurtful legacy and reclaiming your life*. New York: Bantam Books.

Bergland, Cristopher, *Imagination Can Change Perceptions of Reality*, Psychology Today, June 2013.

Orangutan Behavior, "Article", Seaworld.com, Seaworld, http://seaworld. org/animal-info/animal-infobooks/orangutan/behavior/

Hogenboom, Melissa. Chimpanzees can learn to cook, "Article", BBC Magazine, BBC.com, http://www.bbc.com/earth/story/20150603-chimpanzees-can-learn-to-cook, June 2015.

Walker, Matt. Apes reveal the secret to good sleep. "Article", BBC Magazine, BBC.com. April 2015.

J Pers Soc Psychol. 2014 Jul;107(1):122-41. doi: 10.1037/a0036673. Epub 2014 May 12.

Chapter 3

A. Borodin, G. Roberts, J. Rosenthal, and P. Tsaparas. Link analysis ranking: algorithms, theory, and experiments. TOIT, 5:231–297, 2005.

Adams, Paul C. *The Boundless Self: Communication In Physical And Virtual Spaces*, Syracuse University Press, 2005.

B. Zhao, B. I. P. Rubinstein, J. Gemmell, and J. Han. A Bayesian approach to discovering truth from conflicting sources for data integration. PVLDB, 5(6):550–561, 2012.

Brazil, "Article", Wikipedia, https://en.wikipedia.org/wiki/ Brazil_(1985_film).

Georg Simmel, "Article", Wikipedia, https://en.wikipedia.org/wiki/ Georg_Simmel

Guido Möllering, *Trust: Reason, Routine, Reflexivity*, Oxford: Elsevier, 2006, ISBN 0-08-044855-0, Max Planck Institute for the Study of Societies, Paulstr. 3, 50676 Cologne, Germany.

J. Pasternack and D. Roth. Making better informed trust decisions with generalized fact-finding. In IJCAI, pages 2324–2329, 2011.

Kramer, Roderick M. (Ed); Tyler, Tom R. (Ed), (1996). Trust in organizations: Frontiers of theory and research. , (pp. 166-195). Thousand Oaks, CA, US: Sage Publications, Inc, ix, 429 pp.

M. Wu and A. Marian. Corroborating answers from multiple web sources. In Proc. of the WebDB Workshop, 2007.

Mutually Assured Destruction, "Article", Wikipedia: https://en.wikipedia. org/wiki/Mutual_assured_destruction

Reinhard Bachmann, Akbar Zahee (editors), *Handbook of Trust Research*, pp 139, Edward Elgar Publishing, 2008.

Rivera, Joseph de 1977. *A Structural Theory of the Emotions*. New York: International Universities Press.

Rose-Ackerman, Susan 2001. 'Trust, Honesty and Corruption: Reflection on the Statebuilding Process'. European Journal of Sociology. 42 (3): 526-70.

Rousseau, Denise M. Not so different after all: A crossdiscipline view of trust, Carnegie Mellon University.

Scheff, Thomas J.1988. 'Shame and Conformity: The Deference-Emotion System'. American Sociological Review. 53 (3): 395-406.

Seligman, Adam 1997. *The Problem of Trust*. Princeton, NJ: Princeton University Press.

Simmel, Georg 1964. *The Sociology of Georg Simmel*, edited by Kurt H. Wolff. New York: Free Press.

Simmel, Georg. *The Nature of Trust: From Georg Simmel to a Theory of Expectation, Interpretation and Suspension.*

Swift Trust Theory, "Article", Wikipedia, https://en.wikipedia.org/wiki/ Swift_trust_theory.

Trust and knowledge sharing: A critical combination, IBM Institute for Knowledge-Based Organizations, IBM, 2002.

X. Yin, J. Han, and P. S. Yu. Truth discovery with multiple conflicting information providers on the web. In Proc. of SIGKDD, 2007.

Xin Luna Dong et al, Knowledge-Based Trust: Estimating the Trustworthiness of Web Sources, Google Research, 2015.

ZAPPEN, J.P., HARRISON, T. M., and WATSON, D. 2008. A new paradigm for designing e-government: Web2.0 and experience design. In Proceedings of the International Conferenceon Digital Government Research. Digital Government Society of NorthAmerica, 17–26.

ZARGHAMI, A., FAZEL I, S., DOKOOHAKI, N., and MATSKIN, M. 2009. Social trust-aware recommendation system: AI index approach. In Proceedings of the IEEE/WIC/ACM International Joint Conference on Web Intelligence and Intelligent Agent Technology (WIIAT'09). IEEE Computer Society, Los Alamitos, CA, 85–90.

ZHANG, Y., CHEN, H., and WU, Z. 2006. A social network based trust model for the semantic web. In Proceedings of the 6th International Conference on Autonomic and Trusted Computing. 183–192.

Chapter 4

Americans and Social Trust: Who, Where and Why, "Survey", Pew Research, February 2007.
and Company, 43-55.

Apple Passes Coca-Cola as Most Valuable Brand, "Article", New York Times, September, 2013.

Atlas, S., Putterman, L., 2009. Trust among the Avatars: Playing Trust Games in a Virtual World, with and without Textual and Visual Cues. Unpublished Working Paper, Brown University.

Bainbridge, Jane, Taxing issues for marketing as brand trust is called into question, Marketing Magazine, December 2012.

Bainbridge, W., 2007. The scientific research potential of virtual worlds. Science 317(5837), 472-476.

Bowers, Simon, Amazon to begin paying corporation tax on UK retail sales, The Guardian, May 2015.

C. Castelfranchi, Social Power: a missed point in DAI, MA and HCI. In Decentralized AI. Y. Demazeau & J.P.Mueller (eds) (Elsevier, Amsterdam 1991) 49-62.

Castelfranchi, C., Conte, R., Limits of economic and strategic Rationality for Agents and M-A Systems. Robotics and Autonomous Systems, Special issue on Multi-Agent Rationality, Elsevier Editor, Vol 24, Nos 3- 4, , pp.127-139.

Cristiano Castelfranchi and Rino Falcone, Social Trust: A Cognitive Approach, National Research Council - Institute of Psychology, Unit of "AI, Cognitive Modelling and Interaction" Roma – Italy.

"For research and design", International Journal of Human-Computer Studies, 6, 381-422.

Garside, Juliette. Amazon UK boycott urged after retailer pays just £4.2m in tax, The Guardian, May 2014.

Henriques, Diana, B. Scenes From the Madoff Masquerade, New York Times, April 2011.

Kramer, Roderick, Rethinking Trust, Harvard Business Review, pp 69-77, June, 2009.

"Lack of information", Journal of Consumer Research, 19 (3), 412-24.

"Marketing", Journal of Marketing, 58 (July), 20-38.

Mayer, R.C., Davis, J. and Schoorman, D. (1995), "An integrative model of organizational trust", Academy of Management Review, Vol. 20 No. 3, pp. 709-34.

Mitchell, P., Reast, J. and Lynch, J. (1998), "Exploring the foundations of trust", Journal of Marketing Management, Vol. 14, pp. 159-72.

Mizel, Jonathan. Just Go Fishing, "Article", 2013. http://www.jonathanmizel.com/just-go-fishing/#more-301

Monroe, Kent B. and Petroshius, Susan, M. (1981), "Buyers' Perceptions of Price: An Update

Morgan, R.M. and Hunt, S.D. (1994), "The commitment-trust theory of relationship marketing", Journal of Marketing, Vol. 58 No. 3, pp. 20-38.

Morgan, Robert M. and Hunt, Shelby D. (1994), "The commitment-trust theory of relationship of the Evidence, "Perspectives in Consumer Behavior, eds. Glenview, IL: Scott, Foresman

Rao, Akshay and Bergen, Mark (1992), "Price premium variations as a consequence of buyers'

Riegelsberger, J., Sasse, M.A., McCarthy, J.D. (2005), "The mechanics of trust: A framework"

Rosenberg, Matt. Brands: Consumers Don't Want to Be Your BFF in Social (They Want Help), "Article", Ad Age, 2014.

Rotter, J. (1980), "Interpersonal trust, trustworthiness, and gullibility", American Psychologist, Vol. 35, pp. 1-17.

Schurr, P. and Ozanne, J.L. (1985), "Influences on exchange processes: buyers' preconceptions of a seller's trustworthiness and bargaining toughness", Journal of Consumer Research, Vol. 11 No. 4, pp. 939-53.

Sirgy, J. (1982), "Self-concept in consumer behavior: a critical review", Journal of Consumer Research, Vol. 9 No. 3, pp. 287-300

Syrus, Publilius, "The Moral Sayings of Publius Syrus, a Roman Slave: From the Latin" Archive.org. https://archive.org/stream/moralsayingspub00lymagoog/moralsayingspub00lymagoog_djvu.txt

We want to be your friend, "Article", The Economist, February 2014.

Wright, Mic. Brands aren't your friends, they're the idiots at the social media party, "Article", The Next Web, Next Web Inc., July, 2009.

Chapter 5

Atlas, S., Putterman, L., 2009. Trust among the Avatars: Playing Trust Games in a Virtual World, with and without Textual and Visual Cues. Unpublished Working Paper, Brown University.

Bainbridge, W., 2007. The scientific research potential of virtual worlds. Science 317(5837), 472-476.

Blattberg, Robert C. and Neslin, Scott A. (1990), "Sales Promotion: Concepts, Methods, and Strategies, 1st ed., Englewood Cliffs, NJ: Prentice

Hall.

Chaudhuri A. Holbrook M.B. The chain of effects from brand trust and brand affect to brand performance: The role of brand loyalty. Journal of Marketing 2001; 65 (April): 81-93.

Chen, S.C., Dhillon, G.S. (2003), "Interpreting dimensions of consumer trust in e-commerce", Information Technology and Management, 4, 203-318.

Corritore, C.L., Kracher, B., Wiedenbeck, S. (2003), "Online trust : Concepts, evolving themes, a model", International Journal of Human Computer Studies, 58, 737-758.

Johnson-George, C., Swap, W.C. (1982), "Measurement of specific interpersonal trust: Construction and validation of a scale to assess trust in a specific other", Journal of Personality and Social Psychology, 43 (6), 1306-1317.

Kapferer, J.N. and Laurent, G. (1985), "Brand sensitivity: a new concept for brand management", Proceedings of the Annual Conference of the European Marketing Academy.

Mano, Haim and Oliver, Richard, L. (1993), "Assessing the dimensionality and structure of the consumption experience: Evaluation, feeling, and satisfaction", Journal of Consumer Research, 20 (December), 451-466.

Osborne, Alistair, Nicholas Levene: The golden fleecers, The Telegraph, November, 2012.

Chapter 6

Blythe, Jim, Sales and Key Account Management, Union Carbide and Bhopal.

Burghardt Raymond F., Old Enemies Become Friends: U.S. and Vietnam, Brookings, November 2006.

Claser, Edward M.; H. H. Abelson; and K. N. Garrison. Putting Knowledge to Use. San Francisco: Josey-Bass Publishers, 1983.

Deutsch, M. "Trust and Suspicion." Journal of Conflict Resolution, (1958): 265-279.

Giffin, K. "The Contribution of Studies of Source Credibility to a Theory of Interpersonal Trust in the Communication Process." Psychological Bulletin 68, 2 (1967): 104-120.

Heimer, Carol. "Uncertainty and Vulnerability in Social Relations." Unpublished paper. University of Chicago, 1976.

Michell, P. C. "Accord and Discord in Agency-Client Perceptions of Creativity." Journal of Advertising Research 24, 5 (1984): 9-24.

R. L. Burgess and T. L. Huston, eds. New York: Academic Press, 1979. Rotter, Julian B. "A New Scale for the Measurement of Interpersonal Trust." Journal of Personality 35, 4 (1967): 651-665.

Scanzoni, J. "Social Exchange and Behavioral Interdependence." In Social Exchange in Developing Relationships.

Shapiro, Susan P. "The Social Control of Impersonal Trust." American Journal of Sociology 93, 3 (1987): 623-658.

Wackman, D. B.; C. T. Salmon; and C. C. Salmon. "Developing an Advertising Agency-Client Relationship." Journal of Advertising Research 26, 6 (1986): 21-2.

Book 3

Chapter 1

Hodson, H (2014). The AI Boss that Deploys Hong Kong's Subway Engineers. New Scientist

Irani, L., & Silberman, M. (2013). Turkopticon:Interrupting Worker Invisibility in Amazon Mechanical

Isaacs, E., Walendowski, A., Whittaker, S., ...& Kamm, C. (2002). The character, functions, and styles of instant messaging in the workplace. In Proc. of CSCW, 11-20.

Kantor, J. (2014). Working Anything But 9 to 5. NYT

Kay, J. & Kummerfeld, B. (2012). Creating personalized systems that people can scrutinize and control: Drivers, principles and experience. TiiS, 24-42.

Kulesza, T., Stumpf, S., Burnett, M., & Kwan, I. (2012). Tell me more: the effects of mental model soundness on personalizing an intelligent agent. In Proc. of CHI, 1-10.

Lee, J., & Moray, N. (1992). Trust, control strategies and allocation of function in human-machine systems. Ergonomics, 35(10), 1243-1270.

Lee, M. K., Kiesler, S., Forlizzi, J., & Rybski, P. (2012). Ripple effects of an embedded social agent: a field study of a social robot in the workplace. In Proc. of CHI, 695-704.

Lim, B. Y., Dey, A. K., & Avrahami, D. (2009). Why and why not explanations improve the intelligibility of context-aware intelligent systems. In Proc. of CHI, 2119-2128.

ZAPPEN, J. P., HARRISON, T. M., AND WATSON, D. 2008. A new paradigm for designing e-government: Web 2.0 and experience design. In Proceedings of the International Conference on Digital Government Research. Digital Government Society of North America, 17–26.

ZARGHAMI, A., FAZELI, S., DOKOOHAKI, N., AND MATSKIN, M. 2009. Social trust-aware recommendation system: A t-index approach. In Proceedings of the IEEE/WIC/ACM International Joint Conference on Web Intelligence and Intelligent Agent Technology (WI-IAT'09). IEEE Computer Society, Los Alamitos, CA, 85–90.

ZHANG, Y. AND FANG, Y. 2007. A fine-grained reputation system for reliable service selection in peer-to-peer networks. IEEE Trans. Parallel Distrib. Syst. 18, 8, 1134–1145.

ZHANG, Y., CHEN, H., AND WU, Z. 2006. A social network-based trust model for the semantic web. In Proceedings of the 6th International Conference on Autonomic and Trusted Computing. 183–192.

Chapter 2

A. Armstrong and J. Hagel III. The real value of online communities. Harvard Business Review, pages 134–141, 1996.

B. Misztal. Trust in Modern Societies: The Search for the Bases of Social Order. Polity Press, 1996.

Beck, Julie, Digital Romance: The Teens Get It, The Atlantic, 2015.

Epistolary Novel, "Article", Wikipedia, https://en.wikipedia.org/wiki/
Epistolary_novel

J. Golbeck, B. Parsia, and J. Hendler. Trust Networks on the Semantic Web.
In Proc. of CoopIS, 2003.

L. Capra. Engineering human trust in mobile system collaborations. In Proc.
of FSE, 2004.

M. Dell'Amico. Neighbourhood Maps: Decentralised Ranking in Small-
World P2P Networks. In Proc. of HotP2P, 2006.

M. Gladwell. The Tipping Point, How Little Things Can Make a Big
Difference. Little Brown, 2000.

M. Richardson, R. Agrawal, and P. Domingos. Trust management for the
semantic web. In Proceedings of the Second International Semantic Web
Conference, pages 351–368, 2003.

P. Sztompka. Trust: A Sociological Theory. Cambridge University Press,
1999.

R. Levien and A. Aiken. Attack-resistant trust metrics for public key
certification. In Proc. of USENIX Security, 1998.

S. D. Kamvar, M. T. Schlosser, and H. Garcia-Molina. The Eigentrust
algorithm for reputation management in P2P networks. In Proc. of ACM
WWW, 2003.

Victorian Era, "Article", Wikipedia, https://en.wikipedia.org/wiki/
Victorian_era

Index